To Stan
With m...

Xmas 1999.

Memories
of
Bedford

Part of the
Memories
series

The Publishers would like to thank the following companies for
supporting the production of this book

Main Sponsor
Bedford College

Autoglass (UK) Limited

Philip A Barnes Limited

Beavis

Bedfordia Group plc

Bedford High School

Binney & Smith (Europe) Limited

George Fischer Castings Limited

Goldings of Bedford Limited

Hatters

J Hinckley & Sons

Hunting Engineering

Kingston Windows

Krupp Camford

Neville Funeral Service Limited

Rolls Royce Power Engineering plc

Sharman & Trethewy Solicitors

K Watson Limited

Charles Wells Limited

First published in Great Britain by True North Books Limited
Units 3 - 5 Heathfield Industrial Park
Elland West Yorkshire
HX5 9AE
Tel. 01422 377977
© Copyright: True North Books Limited 1999

ISBN 1 900463 83 0

Text, design and origination by True North Books Limited
Printed and bound by The Amadeus Press Limited

Memories are made of this

Memories. We all have them; some good, some bad, but our memories of the town we grew up in are usually tucked away in a very special place in our minds. The best are usually connected with our childhood and youth, when we longed to be grown up and paid no attention to adults who told us to enjoy being young, as these were the best years of our lives. We look back now and realise that they were right.

So many memories - perhaps of the war and rationing, perhaps of parades, celebrations, Royal visits and sporting triumphs. And so many changes; one-way traffic systems and pedestrianisation. New trends in shopping that led to the very first self-service stores being opened.

Through the bad times and the good, however, Bedford not only survived but prospered. We have only to look at the town as it is today, with its finest buildings restored to their full glory, and now complemented by up-to-the-minute facilities, to see what progress has been realised and what achievements have been made over the last 50 years. Bedford has a history to be proud of - but more importantly, a great future to look forward to, into the new millennium and beyond.

Contents

Around the town centre

Shopping jokes in the second half of the 20th century usually centre on Moscow. Spot a woman who has stopped to look up at a passing cloud and a queue immediately forms behind her. Russia does not know that the practice seems to have started in Silver Street. On 6 May 1941, food, clothing and most items vital to normal everyday life were in short supply. If the housewife heard that something she needed had suddenly appeared in the shops, then she dropped everything to head down town before it disappeared from the shelves. Unfortunately, all other holders of the housekeeping purse thought the same. Rationing was necessary to try to make sure that there was a fair distribution of consumer goods that were in short supply. It gave some equality, but also meant that there would always be a black market for those willing and able to pay over the odds for their extra meat, petrol or whatever was on offer. The queues were full of women and children waiting patiently in line. There was no pushing and shoving. It wasn't the British way. Few men joined in. Shopping was women's work. Not that there were large numbers of menfolk around. They were away fighting for King and country. Ezra Braggins' outfitters shop had been here since before 1900. It replaced the general dealer, Brooks French. Mr Archibald Braggins was Mayor of Bedford when war broke out. Reputations count for little. It is not this store that demands the attention of shoppers. Perhaps the butcher further along has some nice sausages in. He will need plenty to satisfy this multitude.

Bottom: The crowded High Street, looking north away from St Paul's Square is so full of shoppers that they have to spill onto the carriageway. The Red Lion is on the east side of the street. To be included in the list of hotels with appointment to the Royal Automobile Club and Automobile Association was a sign of reliable accommodation. Rival patrolmen of the RAC and AA were a common sight on our roads, either side of the war. Firstly on bicycles and then on motorbike and sidecar, they used to salute the motorist member as he approached. The good-mannered greeting was later to be banned in the interests of road safety. Not much need for them on Bedford's town centre streets in 1945. Foot-power, not horsepower, got you around. Clothing styles of different age groups were interesting. Younger women had started to do away with the need to wear a hat in public. This was partly down to their greater acceptance as equals in the workplace. Their wartime contributions had shown that they could carry out traditional men's jobs. Consequently, there was less need to be demure in public. Men showed change, firstly, through their choice of headgear. The flat cap of the older and more working-class man vied with the trilby of the younger or more raffish chap. Even more modern males went bareheaded. Even so, there was a clinging to tradition in wearing a collar and tie in public.

Right: As the war drew to a close, the sight of army and air force vehicles on High Street would soon be a thing of the past. We had grown accustomed to the American bombers flying over our heads on their way to attack German cities. It was only a matter of six weeks before this photograph was taken that the February 1945 raid on Dresden had seen 400 B-17s join our Lancasters in reducing the city to ruins. 'Bomber' Harris's terror campaign of destroying the enemy's will to fight was as

controversial then as it remains now, over 50 years later. Anxiously waiting to cross the road towards Mill Street, the lady in the long coat and bucket hat has her little basket of eggs to carry safely to the other side. She could deposit them in the National Westminster bank over there, for they were in such short supply as to be worth their weight in gold. How she contrasts with the woman immediately behind her, heading towards the corner of the EP Rose and Son's store before turning into Silver Street. Her high heels, nylon stockings, short coat and fashionable hat, atop a perfectly permed coiffure, stamp her as a woman of the future. The flat shoes and 'Norah Batty' stockings of the basket carrier mark her as one of days gone by. Beyond the lights was the 50 Shilling Tailor. Every town had one. Buying a suit for to-day's decimal equivalent of £2.50 seems laughable to the modern snappy dresser, but at least we wore suits then, not some scruffy garb of T shirt and jeans or the all purpose tracksuit and trainers.

The market is in full swing on St Paul's Square. To the east across the tops of the stalls, Lloyds Bank dominates the view. The picture was taken from near the Corn Exchange. The popular American Glenn Miller Band had played at the Corn Exchange only six months before the date of this photograph. His 'String of Pearls' and 'Chatanooga Choo-Choo' had been played to Bedford audiences on many occasions. It was from here that many of his morale-boosting concerts were broadcast and was home to the much-missed musician when he stayed in England. A plaque on the wall, placed there in 1994, commemorates the 50th anniversary of his death on 15 December 1944, when his plane disappeared on a flight to Paris. His life story was told on film in the Glenn Miller Story, a box office smash of 1953. James Stewart played the part of the bandleader. As the woman looks towards the Corn Exchange which had stood since Russell Hasting, 9th Duke of Bedford opened it, in 1874, what thoughts are going through her head? Is it a wistful look of nostalgia as she recalls the trombonist leading his band into the romantic 'Moonlight Serenade' or the rousing chorus of 'Pennsylvania Six, Five, Thousand'? Life has to go on and there is shopping to be done over the road. But, surely, she can be allowed a moment to remember the 40 year old whose like will never be seen again. Glenn's place in history is safe.

Servicemen mix with civilians in High Street at the Mill Street and Silver Street crossroads. During World War II, the sons and daughters of Bedford served with distinction. The cause was not without its casualties. In February 1942, men from the County Regiment were captured at Singapore. Over 200 did not return, while others spent long, harrowing years as Japanese prisoners of war. Some never recovered from the experience. None ever forgot. The Bedfordshire and Hertfordshire Regiment no longer exists as a separate force. It is now part of the Royal Anglian Regiment, formed in 1964 from the regiments of the East Anglian Brigade, which themselves had been created through a series of amalgamations of former county regiments between 1958 and 1960. The Taylor, Brawn and Flood building on the left is now the Cooper Beard estate agency. Shoppers stream into the great department store of EP Rose and Son.

The Bedfordshire Times used to carry a weekly advert for the store in a prominent place on its pages. The size and power of the call to shop at Rose's overshadowed any message from its competitors. But, nothing lasts forever. It is now the name of Debenham's that adorns this building. In 1945, there was a spring in the step of the shoppers going about their day's affairs. A light was appearing on the horizon. It was called 'peace'. Soon, it would belong to everyone, service personnel and civilians alike.

A glance at the 1930s

WHAT'S ON?
In this heyday of the cinema, horrified audiences were left gasping at the sight of Fay Wray in the clutches of the giant ape in the film 'King Kong', released in 1933. Very different but just as gripping was the gutsy 1939 American Civil War romance 'Gone with the Wind'. Gable's parting words, 'Frankly, my dear, I don't give a damn' went down in history.

GETTING AROUND
At the beginning of the decade many believed that the airship was the transport of the future. The R101 airship, however, loaded with thousands of cubic metres of hydrogen, crashed in France on its maiden flight in 1930. Forty-eight passengers and crew lost their lives. In 1937 the Hindenburg burst into flames - the entire disaster caught on camera and described by a distraught reporter. The days of the airship were numbered.

SPORTING CHANCE
The black American Jesse Owens won a brilliant four world records in the 1936 Olympic Games in Berlin, thumbing the nose to Adolf Hitler's dreams of Aryan superiority. In a petty display Hitler walked out of the stadium and 'took his bat home'; later he refused to have his photograph taken with the victorious Owens.

Above: Unless you know the shops on Silver Street, it would be difficult to date this panorama. The clothing of the people busying themselves around the assorted retail outlets might give a clue. The lack of vehicles, just cyclists making their way towards the camera, should tell you that it was an era when fuel was scarce. It is April 1945. We are looking across High Street from Mill Street, westward down Silver Street which was pedestrianised in 1985. New paving was supplied. Tree planting and provision of raised flowerbeds made it more pleasing to the eye. It was intended to create a meeting and focal point at one of the busiest parts of town. In the evening, it has created a skateboard and cycling arena for the teens, but this was hardly in the mind of the planners. Lilley and Skinner on the left, became Saxone's shoe shop, but that closed in 1990 and is now The Body Shop. Thomson's butchers does not sell its chops and steaks from this prime spot any more. The clothing store, Next, now occupies this building. Its side elevation has not changed. Neither has that of Burton's, on the right. In fact, the famous tailor still clothes Bedford men to this day. Over five decades ago, the store would soon be preparing to kit out returning servicemen in their demob suits, or 'full Monty' as they were affectionately known. Burton's has brought a number of sayings into our language. It was once said that someone was so lucky that, if he fell off Burton's roof, he would land inside a new suit!

Above right: This northern side of Midland Road has changed very little since 1945. British Home Stores and Woolworth's still carry on business either side of James Street. Marks and Spencer continues to occupy pride of place, on the corner of Harpur Street. Until 1929, the White Horse had sold Jarvis and Company's ales on the site. Even Boot's chemist store remains here, though it has moved a few yards from the right of M&S to a place just over the photographer's shoulder. It is on the south side of the street that the major shopping change has come. The new shopping mall, the Harpur Centre, has been built on the site of the former Bedford Modern School. Designed in 1831, it is a major work of architect Edward Blore. It combined the Commercial School, Harpur Hospital (Orphanage), the Harpur Trust boardroom and offices as well as the Elementary School. The school left the building in 1974. Sir Frederick Gibberd designed the replacement shopping centre, keeping the entrance facade of the school as a historical link. This section of Midland Road is now part of the pedestrianised centre of Bedford. Changes in shopping patterns lay ahead for those out and about as the middle of the 20th century approached. The first half had brought its own developments. FW Woolworth, the pioneer of the five and ten cent store, had brought his cheap and cheerful approach to England in the early 1900s, opening a store in Liverpool in 1909. 'Marks and Sparks' opened a store in Wigan around 1913 and soon established the chain in most of our towns.

This 1945 street scene was captured in High Street, looking north. On the east side of the street the golden bull and its clock still look across the traffic and pedestrians scurrying below them to-day. Nowadays, the optician's shop, Allder's, does business under the famous landmark. The bull advertised John Bull, jeweller and it has now been there for over a century. Erected by Thomas Bull in 1884, it caused some annoyance to the aesthetic eye of some of the Bedfordian diehards. Mr Bull was reported as saying, 'I am quite satisfied with it'. It was a clever advert for his jeweller's shop as well as providing an amenity for the town. Controversy about it rumbled on for years. Thomas Bull's successors have moved the business to St Peter's, but his golden namesake (a replica of the original) continues to provide a talking point for visitors to the town. Shopping in Bedford has always been a fairly comfortable exercise. The town centre and its immediate vicinity are quite level and flat. There was no puffing and blowing up steep inclines or heavy work on the bicycle's old Sturmey-Archer gears for shoppers then or now. Many locals still use the pushbike as a means of getting around the centre. In places, there are special cycle lanes. There are also pavements that the modern day Reg Harris bowls along, so watch out when on the so-called pedestrianised areas.

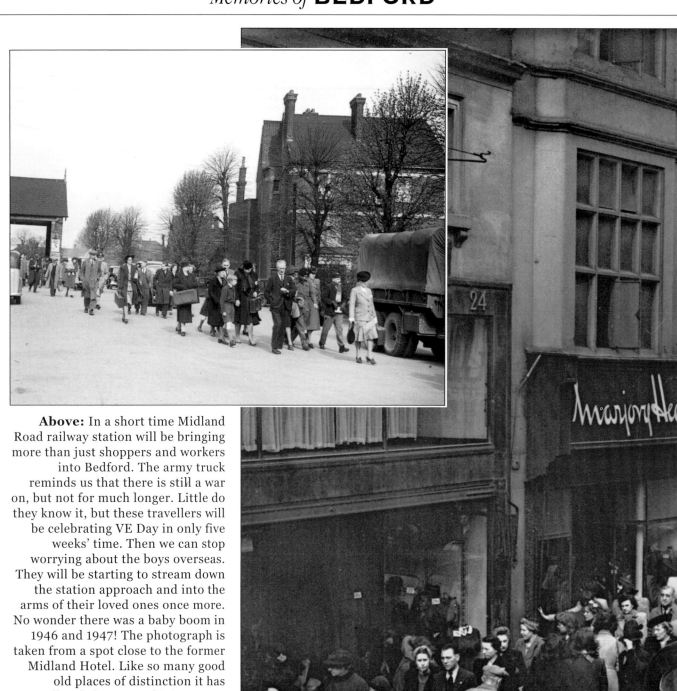

Above: In a short time Midland Road railway station will be bringing more than just shoppers and workers into Bedford. The army truck reminds us that there is still a war on, but not for much longer. Little do they know it, but these travellers will be celebrating VE Day in only five weeks' time. Then we can stop worrying about the boys overseas. They will be starting to stream down the station approach and into the arms of their loved ones once more. No wonder there was a baby boom in 1946 and 1947! The photograph is taken from a spot close to the former Midland Hotel. Like so many good old places of distinction it has suffered change, and it is now an Irish theme pub. Ashburnham Road runs off to the right, behind the formerly Waverley Temperance Hotel, carrying people out towards the road to Northampton and such villages as Turvey and Bromham. The old station was replaced in 1978 by the new Midland Station 100 yards further north, and by 1999, Thameslink could speed you into London's King's Cross in a matter of 50 minutes. Many people commute daily. Even Gatwick is only 90 minutes away for the jetsetters who have been attracted to make their homes in the more exclusive environs of Bedford.

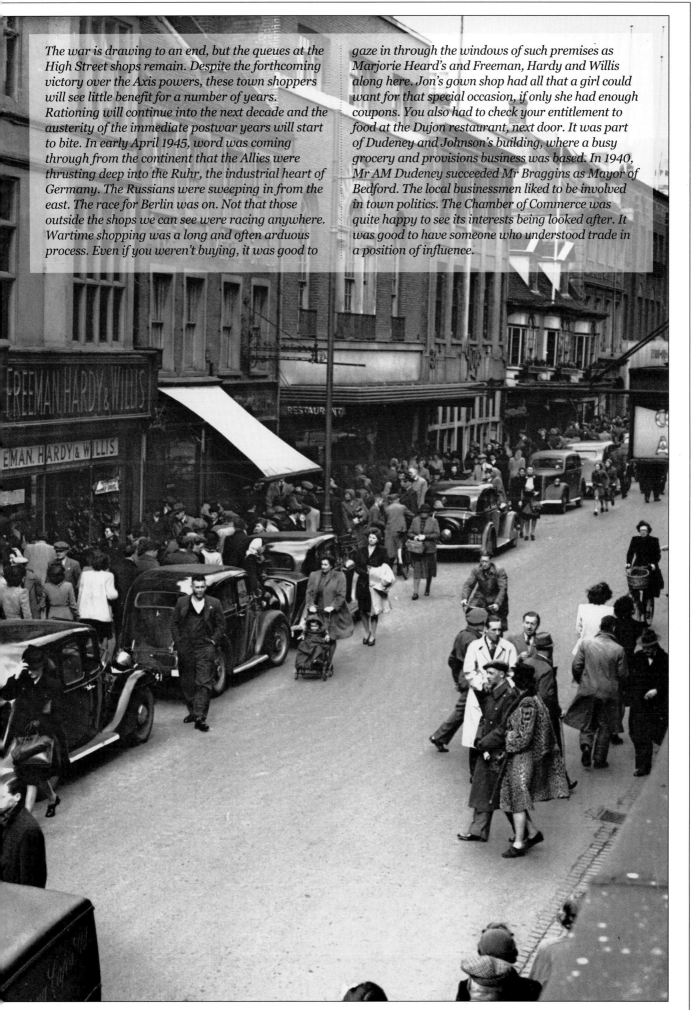

The war is drawing to an end, but the queues at the High Street shops remain. Despite the forthcoming victory over the Axis powers, these town shoppers will see little benefit for a number of years. Rationing will continue into the next decade and the austerity of the immediate postwar years will start to bite. In early April 1945, word was coming through from the continent that the Allies were thrusting deep into the Ruhr, the industrial heart of Germany. The Russians were sweeping in from the east. The race for Berlin was on. Not that those outside the shops we can see were racing anywhere. Wartime shopping was a long and often arduous process. Even if you weren't buying, it was good to gaze in through the windows of such premises as Marjorie Heard's and Freeman, Hardy and Willis along here. Jon's gown shop had all that a girl could want for that special occasion, if only she had enough coupons. You also had to check your entitlement to food at the Dujon restaurant, next door. It was part of Dudeney and Johnson's building, where a busy grocery and provisions business was based. In 1940, Mr AM Dudeney succeeded Mr Braggins as Mayor of Bedford. The local businessmen liked to be involved in town politics. The Chamber of Commerce was quite happy to see its interests being looked after. It was good to have someone who understood trade in a position of influence.

At leisure

Left: School dinners and the delight of soggy mash, over-boiled cabbage and greasy stew was the enduring memory we all have of lunchtime at school. You knew if it was roly-poly pud for afters if the cook was only wearing one stocking. Otherwise it was semolina. Yuk! Well, it was not like that at St John's Nursery. These ladies took a serious view of nutrition. They were putting into practice what the NHS preached. Give the youngsters a healthy, balanced diet. For some, dinner would be the only hot meal they would get that day. Means testing made sure that the needy got their school meal free, even though there was a stigma attached to being one of those with a letter 'F' after your name in the register. As the 1950s drew to a close, the health drive was still on. The battle against the spread of tuberculosis in urban areas, made worse by poor sanitation and hygiene, was being won. The BCG immunisation programme was a success. The Salk vaccine controlled polio, a killer and crippler in the 1940s. Even so, the Ministry of Health took its responsibility seriously. Sedate housewives were warned about the dangers of obesity. That went down well with the women on their hands and knees scrubbing floors and donkey-stoning steps. They were also warned about the addictive nature of sedatives and tranquilisers. It was a pity that the advice did not stretch to the prescribing of thalidomide in 1959.

Below: Now then, Leonardo, what shall we create to-day? Perhaps a portrait of that grumbling girl at the next easel. We could call it 'Moaner Lisa'. Maybe not, it would never catch on. No time for idle thoughts or flights of fancy for these lads at St John's Day Nursery in the summer of 1959. Forty years ago the sun shone in June. At least it did on this day. Off into the great outdoors and make as much mess as you like. 'Tell me about your picture,' the teacher would say. It was better than 'That's nice, what is it?' That meant the same, but was not quite as obvious. Powder paints, potato prints and cuttin' and stickin' were the ways we expressed our artistic souls. There is not a vat of formaldehyde or a pile of bricks in sight. Finish this painting and 'miss' will clip it onto the line to dry. Come the end of the day and we can show it to Mum. She will tell us how clever we are and put it up on our bedroom wall. These were the days when you could be politically incorrect and call the playhouse a Wendy house. Boys played with Dinky cars, imagining they were Stirling Moss. The girls had their dollies and pushed them in prams down to the imaginary shops. Play was important in learning and finding out how to mix with others. Forty years on, four year olds have to be graded and tested under the National Curriculum. There is no time to be a child any more.

Above: The summer of 1966 was a glorious one in many ways. The national soccer team had won the World Cup. The late Sir Alf Ramsey had delivered what he had promised. 'They think it's all over. It is now.' But, not for the Bedford Carnival, it wasn't. Thoughts of stirring deeds on the football field were far away as these youngsters enjoyed their day out. Racing along mini railways, throwing rings at the hoopla stall and trying to knock off coconuts that had been cemented onto their bases were joys to be had. If they were really lucky there would be another goldfish in a jam jar to bring home and amuse the cat as she stuck her paw inside the bowl and tried to flip it out. The more serious minded could watch a demonstration of lace making on those glass-spangled bobbins. St John's Ambulance Brigade members were on hand to help out with the occasional sprained ankle and the tannoy would announce the name of some tearful toddler who had become separated from her mum. We watched the processions and loved the costumes that people had stitched, sewed and fretted over for weeks before. Thank goodness the rain kept away, for that was the only possible damper to a great day out. In the background, the band was playing the 'Floral Dance' and the theme to the 1965 film 'Those Magnificent Men in their Flying Machines', just to show there was something modern in its repertoire.

Above right: Is it a bird? Is it a plane? Is it the Loch Ness monster? No, it is a frogman. Members of the police diving team are putting on an exhibition at the Bedford Water Carnival. Fascinated by the skill of these divers, hundreds lined The Embankment to see the oxygen tanks bob up and down through the waters of the Great Ouse as they went through their paces. The river has played a central role in the town's history. As it was fordable in earlier times, the Saxon chief Beda founded a settlement near here. So, the name of Bedford or Beda's Ford, came into being. After William the Conqueror arrived on our shores in 1066, a castle was built by the river, which in the late 17th century was made navigable as far as King's Lynn and gave access to the sea for the town's merchants. In late Victorian and Edwardian times, much housing was built for the middle classes, largely attracted by the Harpur Trust schools. The attractive Town Bridge and elegant Suspension Bridge across the river date from 1813 and 1888 respectively. In 1998, the Prince of Wales opened the new Butterfly Bridge. Behind the spectators in the picture a glimpse can be caught of the old Picturedrome Cinema. A modern hotel, the Moat House, now stands here. The view from many of its 100 plus bedrooms is one of the most attractive in Bedford.

The day nursery at St John's was one of many centres to be targeted during the 1959 Public Health campaign. It was not because there were any individual concerns about the nursery's level of care, but as one of many public drives to improve the health and fitness of the general public. After the National Health Service was born in 1947, local health authorities provided maternity and child welfare, post-hospital care, home nursing, immunisation, ambulance service and various other preventative and educational services. They also operated clinics, as well as day nurseries for children, such as the one here. Cleanliness is, indeed, next to godliness. If this is true, those words of John Wesley are being well practised here. Which 40 year old reader is now looking at this picture and grimacing at the sight of his or her birthday suit on show to all and sundry? The message was being drummed home to all the children. Wash behind your ears, bathe regularly, clean your teeth and rinse your hands after using the toilet. All these, and more, were ingrained in the upbringing of little ones. Their teachers and nurses had seen only too clearly that the lack of sanitation, dirty living conditions and poor healthcare practices had bred disease in the pre-war years. This was now the age of the Welfare State and scabies, lice and other unmentionables were to be eradicated. Bath time had to be fun, too, so pass the plastic duck and blow some bubbles for me.

On the move

From here, Tavistock Street heads left towards Clapham, and Bromham Road to Northampton. On the right are the railings around St Peter's Church. Behind the taxi kiosk on the Broadway, De Parys Avenue, with its wide grass verges and mature trees, leads to the open spaces of Bedford Park. This is one of the most picturesque of the town's residential avenues. Late Victorian and Edwardian houses belong to an age of well-to-do middle classes with their maids and cooks in residence. These days, some of the residences are small hotels or guesthouses, close enough to the town for convenience, but quietly tucked away from the main hustle and bustle. Standing proudly at the

nerve centre of the taxi company is Mr Edwin Crawley. By 1960, Edwin had been here almost as long as Bunyan's Statue, or so it seemed. Even if he had not taken root here, he was still able to claim that he was Bedford's oldest cabbie. Born in the 19th century, he had seem some developments. As a lad he had travelled in the pony and trap age, when the brougham, hansom and victoria cabs were the forerunners of the hackney carriages he would drive. The inscription on the statue could have been placed at his feet - 'The law of truth was written upon his lips; it stood as if it pleaded with men'. Erected in 1908, the kiosk was demolished 60 years later.

Below: Wrapped up against the cold of January 1959, this lady is going through the ritual of the punched ticket at Midland Road Station. How many hundreds did he clip in a day? Maybe she was off on a shopping trip to the capital. If so, it was a quick and comfortable journey. Spare a thought for Catherine Young. In 1833 she took 12 hours to get to London by coach. It also cost a shilling to send a letter there. By 1848 she could make the journey by train in 2 1/2 hours for just 5s 3d. The coach fare was a guinea (£1 1s). Her letter went for a penny. At those prices and at that speed it was no surprise that the railway swept all competition aside. It would not be until the coming of motor transport in the 20th century that any challenge would be mounted. A burst of activity in 1905 saw new stations built as rail bosses recognised the threat.

Bottom: As the Second World War drew to a close, public transport was an important part of our lives. Car ownership was not the norm and we relied on the bus and train to get us to work and back. Those fortunate enough to possess a motor car had little petrol to run it, so tight was the rationing allocation. Broadway Omnibus Station, to give it the official title, was the hub from which all the services to the outlying parishes ran. Just beyond the terminus was the Dolphin pub where we could call for a quick one before we took the journey home. Other than something alcoholic, the picture brings back memories of that typically British product, Bovril. The Bovril factory was near Ampthill, to the south of Bedford. No winter's day was complete without hands in mittens clasped around a steaming mug of the beef extract with that peculiar, but oh so special, taste. Strong men could not stand for 90 minutes on the football terraces without relying on the mighty Bovril to keep them going. One 1944 advert linked the war and the power of the product. It showed a man sitting astride a barrage balloon. Underneath him was the slogan, 'Bovril prevents that sinking feeling'. Interestingly, the catchphrase was designed before World War I but was held back at the time out of respect for the families of the *Titanic* victims.

Above: Teamwork is the name of the game on British Railways. One to sort and stack, the other to drive. It is not just people that need to be moved around on the tracks. There are goods to be moved on, large and small. There must be some heavy duty cleaning to be done if all those packs of Ajax are to be got through. The cleanser was named after the Greek god who was second only in strength and bravery to Achilles. It was a good choice to inspire a sense of power in the product. Our two railway workers were not too worried about mythology. They were more concerned in getting their stores and parcels moved on efficiently. A century before had seen the goods service provided by the new-fangled railway start a major challenge to the canal system of moving products around the country. The horse-drawn carts had already proved to be too slow and too small to deal with the volume needed to be transported in the 19th century. The Duke of Bridgewater and his engineer, James Brindley, had pioneered canal transport at Worsley, Lancashire, in the 1760s. By 1830 there were 5,000 miles of canals. Then came rail. As early as 1844 merchants in Yorkshire found that it cost as much to bring wool by road or water from Leeds to Bradford, a distance of 10 miles, as it did from Hull (58 miles). The heyday of steam was coming. Unfortunately, these 1959 railwaymen were to see the end of that era and the trimming of the rail service in the 1960s.

Below: Every little boy's dream was to drive a steam engine. Second best was to man the signal box and pull the levers and switch the points to send trains on their way to destinations as far afield as London or Edinburgh. It was enough to make your mouth water to think of the power in the hands of the signalman as he pulled and pushed his bewildering selection of handles. He played them like a drummer beating out a rhythm for the band. The nearest we got to it was to lay out the Hornby Double O on the living room floor and lose ourselves in a world of imagined tunnels, embankments and switched tracks. This signal box at Bedford North Junction stayed until 1978 when the new Midland Station opened. A Portakabin replaced it. That only lasted for two years. It was dismantled and moved to Northampton. The saddest part of that story is that the old signal box was destroyed. Whoever was responsible for the decision to do away with the old and keep the new boring shed could not have been a railway enthusiast or lover of history. That person would have had no interest in knowing that there were originally three main trunk routes across Bedfordshire. These were the West Coast Main Line from Euston, the Midland Main Line from St Pancras and the East Coast Line from King's Cross. That, though, would not have moved the philistine who could destroy a piece of history and keep something resembling a portable toilet.

Comics often used to have a joke on the top line of a page. Only if you are over 50 will you understand the joke on the Beano or Dandy that asked 'What is the connection between a railway engine and a smacked child?' Give the answer, 'They both have a tender behind' and those youngsters of the diesel-electric age will look at you nonplussed. They do not remember the days of the coal piled high behind the engine driver's cab and the shovel sticking out of the pile. The fireman lost pounds in weight during every journey, stoking the furnaces under the boiler that drove the iron horse along its tracks. On this January day in 1959 you could travel from Bedford Midland Road to Chesterfield for 14s 9d or to Leicester for a modest 7s 9d. On a Sunday light refreshments were served. What a treat! The station at Bedford St John's advertised journeys to Cambridge at 5s 3d. That is about 26p in to-day's money. Railway buffs, definitely not anoraks, can wallow in thoughts of Black Fives, Midland Compounds and V2s. Who, if old enough, can fail to thrill to the memory of A2s, Jubilees and the fondly remembered Coronations filling the air with clouds of gushing steam as they snaked cross-country to London or Birmingham? Bedford Railway began life in 1846, being the county's first line. The railwaymen here would not be recalling those days. Of more interest would be the closure of Ampthill Station on the Midland Line in May.

Wartime

Below: *Official civil defence groups provided support for the troops on leave or billeted nearby. Other charitable and volunteer organisations played their part, as well. These good ladies of the Rothsay Road Baptist Church are dispensing free refreshments to the servicemen in May 1941. There is a sting in the tail. Although no charge is made, donations to the War Relief Service are asked for. This is quite a neat trick as the lads will probably give more than the value of the snack, rather than appear tight-fisted. At the same time, the Christian message sits boldly above the Corona pop bottles, reminding the men that they must attend to their souls as well as their bodies. In the 17th century, religion came to the forefront of local life.*

After 1660, non-Anglican worship was banned. Attempts were made to suppress independence of spirit and religion.The Independent (or Congregational Church) had an outspoken member in John Bunyon. He was imprisoned for illegal preaching and published 'The Pilgrim's Progress' in 1678, six years after his release. By the middle of the 18th century, there was greater religious tolerance and co-existence. German Moravians, Wesley's Methodists, followers of Calvinism, Nonconformists and Baptists lived their own brand of Protestantism without too much rancour. A statue to John Bunyan stands on The Broadway, looking straight down High Street.

The colours of the King's Battalion are proudly paraded around the town on 20 May 1941. Everything comes to a standstill as vantage points are sought on balconies above the High Street shops, as well as the pavements below. Marching soldiers in the streets have become a common sight, but never one to be ignored. The standards they carried had great significance, because they represented the honour of the regiment. If the standard bearer fell in battle, it was necessary for another to seize it and raise it aloft once more. The lowering or striking of the colours meant surrender. To capture those of the enemy was a major triumph. First used in the Middle Ages by great nobles and monarchs, the standard originally marked the position of an important individual before a battle. The regimental colours developed to be more than a sign of 'where' and became an indication of 'what'. Whenever a regiment fought with distinction, it was authorised to have the name of that battle painted directly on the flag. These battle honours gave the flags increased significance, making them a record of valourous service as well as symbols of home and country. Regiments took great pride in their battle honours and often transferred them to new flags when the old ones were removed from service. In World War II, the Regiment served world-wide. Battalions fought in France in 1940, took part in the heroic defence of Malta, landed in the first few minutes of the D-Day operation and fought in the jungles of Burma.

Russell Park was the venue for the opening of 'Wings for Victory' week in mid-June 1943. Lord Kindersley gave the introductory address and appealed for support from all Bedford folk. It was to be a massive push for financial contributions towards amassing the hardware of war. The enemy was overstretched. Fighting on several fronts, in North Africa, Italy and on the Russian front had left Germany exposed to a concerted counter strike. Mussolini, the Italian dictator, was about to be deposed and Britain needed to prepare to liberate Europe. The country was rejoicing in the events of the previous month when the bouncing bombs of Barnes Wallis had destroyed the Mohne and Eder dams. Coal mines, iron works and a power station were wrecked. The exploits of the 617 Squadron would be immortalised in a hit film in the 1950s. So, it was an appropriate cause which we were being asked to support. Lord Kindersley made the

A glance at the 1940s

WHAT'S ON?
In wartime Britain few families were without a wireless set. It was the most popular form of entertainment, and programmes such as ITMA and Music While You Work provided the people with an escape from the harsh realities of bombing raids and ration books. In 1946 the BBC introduced the Light Programme, the Home Service and the Third Programme, which gave audiences a wider choice of listening.

GETTING AROUND
October 1948 saw the production of Britain's first new car designs since before the war. The Morris Minor was destined for fame as one of the most popular family cars, while the four-wheel-drive Land Rover answered the need for a British-made off-road vehicle.
The country was deeply in the red, however, because of overseas debts incurred during the war. The post-war export drive that followed meant that British drivers had a long wait for their own new car.

SPORTING CHANCE
American World Heavyweight Boxing Champion Joe Louis, who first took the title back in 1937, ruled the world of boxing during the 1940s, making a name for himself as unbeatable. Time after time he successfully defended his title against all comers, finally retiring in 1948 after fighting an amazing 25 title bouts throughout his boxing career. Louis died in 1981 at the age of 67.

most of reminding us of the further efforts we needed to make to ensure that Britain's Spitfires, Hurricanes, Wellingtons and Lancasters continued to fly sorties into Europe and soften resistance to any invasion. The message was over the heads of the youngsters at the bottom right of the picture. Yet, they were the ones for whom the benefits were intended. Their future was the reason we had entered the conflict. It would be to them that we would look, in years to come, for the preservation of peace and the return to prosperity.

Right: But for the sign on top there is little to tell you that this Morrison Shelter is not some form of rabbit hutch for a rather large bunny. The women examining it, on chill January day in 1942, seem both amused and dubious about its value as a lifesaver. Herbert Morrison was a major Labour politician of the 20th century. Leader of the London County Council, he had become a Member of Parliament in 1923. He was deputy leader of the Labour party for 10 years after World War II. He went to the upper house as Lord Morrison of Lambeth in 1959. He died in 1965. During the war, he was Home Secretary in the Coalition Government. He was not responsible for inventing this device, but, as the Minister for Home Security, he approved it and it bore his name. The Blitz on Britain's major cities was in full swing and we did not all have Anderson shelters at the bottom of our gardens or Tube stations to bed down in. This contraption was meant to provide security from the bombs in the confines of our own homes. Although there was something almost Heath Robinson about crawling into this Morrison shelter and expecting to be protected from 500 lb of high explosive crashing through the roof, Bedford's Borough Engineer recommended it. Charles Blakeway said that 'Householders who desire these should apply to my office for the appropriate form. Where no other shelter is reasonably available, these will be issued free to householders, entitled to free shelter, whose income is less than £350 a year. Otherwise they can be purchased at £7 each.' Move the lettuce, bunny, I'm coming in.

Below: The life of a soldier is bedevilled with danger. That is the nature of the job. On the battlefield they must dodge the bullets and avoid the shells. Yet, these men do the opposite. They search out the metal jacketed means of death and destruction. They are members of the Army Bomb Disposal team, on training manoeuvres in September 1941. Teams gathered at Kempston Barracks (as shown here) or the Drill Hall on Ashburnham Road. Nerves of steel and a steady hand were only part of the requirements. Experience and knowledge were of paramount importance. They needed to have familiarity with every type of device that they might meet. In the early days of the war, defusing unexploded bombs was a more straightforward task. As the hostilities continued, newer and trickier problems presented themselves. Delayed detonation cost limbs and lives until rigorous training helped the experts come to terms with the new developments. The detection and destroying of minefields was an added skill to be acquired. Recognising and locating booby traps and trip wires was just part of the job. Years later, similar teams would be deployed in Northern Ireland. Remote controlled machines would help, but the sight of the individual bomb disposal officer crawling towards a suspicious object in his heavily padded suit and head guard is, sadly, still with us. Out in Kosovo, in the summer of 1999, NATO ground troops were led in by men sweeping the roads ahead for evidence of Serbian mines. The appeal for the destruction of landmines, led by the late Princess of Wales, did not reach the ears of Belgrade. Call out these brave lads, again.

Above: All contributions were gratefully accepted. Displayed on the poster on the wall is the massive target that was set. Towns aimed high. Luton was asked to achieve over £1,000,000. In a brief seven-day period, Bedford raised £721,796. That awesome figure works out at £15 13s 9d per head of population. At a time when the average weekly wage was in single figures, it shows the nature of the true Brit. Sacrifice and belt tightening were the watchwords and how well we took them on board. All age groups were involved in scrimping together every penny they could to go towards the final amount. Goldington Green School promised to raise £150. It got £293 10s. London Road Junior School thought it might manage to scrape together £60 to go towards the provision of a lifeboat. It more than doubled its prediction. The children gathered a remarkable £128 0s 6d. Stories of similar generosity and commitment were echoed across the county. Towns and boroughs examined the league tables like a soccer manager under threat of dismissal, so fierce was the competition to be seen to be succeeding. Rushden UDC challenged Bedford by raising £250,000 to fund the destroyer 'Quorn'. It was a case of Rushden's 'Quorn' versus Bedford's 'Thorn'. At one stage, Bedfordshire was the leading county in the race to be top of the charts of those counties with a population of less than 500,000. There was a complex way of calculating the per capita figure and first place was lost. There was some petty bickering over this, but that was far outweighed by the magnificence and importance of the achievement.

Top: In the middle years of World War II there seemed to be 'a week' virtually every fortnight. It was an exaggeration, but there were constant appeals to the general public to fund yet another venture, vital to the country's war effort. This one was 'Warship Week', held at the end of February 1942. Later on we would get 'Wings for Victory' week and 'Salute the Soldier' week. We had already had 'War Weapons' week the year before. In between, there were collections for paper and all sorts of metal salvage items. You could not accuse us of dereliction of duty, however. Admiral Donaldson opened the appeal on 21 February and the band of the Bedfordshire and Hertfordshire Regiment played at a public dance. Forces' members marched past to give a visual encouragement; not that Bedford needed it. Towns all over Britain joined in, though the week chosen for the big fund-raising drive differed a little. To give the drive a competitive edge and increase participation, targets were set and league tables for the results were drawn up. At the opening ceremony, local VIPs sent messages of encouragement. The Lord Lieutenant, Lord Luke, and Sir George Royle, chairman of the Bedford Savings Committee, had stirring words to express. One of the most poignant came from Sir Richard Wells, the Member of Parliament. His son had been killed defending British skies. We were only being asked to give money. His family had made the ultimate sacrifice.

Above: How many of these mothers' sons would be lying cold on some foreign field in the months to come? The war had still some two years to run and the odds against them all returning safe home to Blighty were poor indeed. While many in the crowd looked on with a blind chauvinism, willing the troops on to crush the forces of fascism, others were more guarded. Out there was someone's husband, someone's sweetheart and someone's son. Those old enough to remember the Great War knew that over one third of those who went out came back on a stretcher or in a coffin. Those statistics made you temper your enthusiastic cheers. Bedford saw little direct action in the 1939-45 war. The first air raid warning did not sound until August 1940. Even then, although 20 bombs fell on East Anglia, this town was left alone until the very moment the all clear was sounded. A lone German fighter appeared and strafed a workshop. One man was injured when a bullet caught him in the back. That was the sole incident until a raid on Ashburnham Road and Midland Road on 23rd July 1942. However, all the townspeople were to be touched in some way. Everyone had a relative serving at the front or one who was a city dweller, dodging the nightly bombing raids coming at them from the continent. One of the first of Bedfordshire's famous sons to be lost was Squadron Leader James M Wells, son of Sir Richard and Lady Wells. He was killed in 1940. Enemy gunfire did not differentiate between class and wealth. The rich fell with the poor.

Above right: Oh how we clapped and cheered as we looked on wave after wave of uniforms that passed before us. The sun shone on what should have been a calm summer's day. Along The Embankment, just for that day, it was so. Elsewhere, the King was in Africa, rallying the Allied troops in a morale raising visit. The struggle against the U-boats in the North Atlantic was turning in our favour, as they were withdrawn to counter an invasion Hitler thought might be coming. Some sad news was the death of that fine actor, Leslie Howard. He was on board a civil airliner shot down over the Bay of Biscay. However, we had a lot to be thankful for. The show of strength saw representatives of all those involved in the struggle for a Europe free from tyranny. It was good to see that the volunteer and auxiliary forces marched on an equal footing with soldiers, sailors and pilots. Now it was the turn of the Land Army. If it is true that an army marches on its stomach, then it must be so for those of us left behind in our march towards resisting the deprivations of war. Without the calloused hands and backaches of the girls labouring in the fields, so that food could appear on our plates, we would have caved in long ago. So, come on, three cheers for them and a special round of applause for Buttercup, while you are at it.

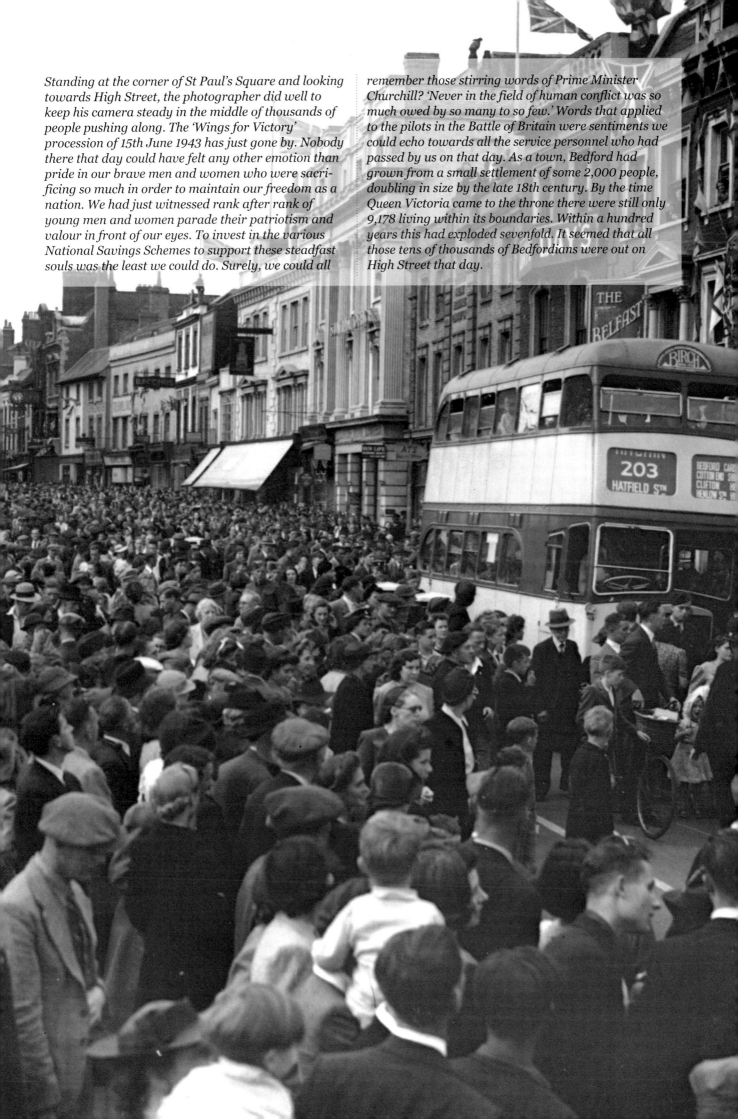

Standing at the corner of St Paul's Square and looking towards High Street, the photographer did well to keep his camera steady in the middle of thousands of people pushing along. The 'Wings for Victory' procession of 15th June 1943 has just gone by. Nobody there that day could have felt any other emotion than pride in our brave men and women who were sacrificing so much in order to maintain our freedom as a nation. We had just witnessed rank after rank of young men and women parade their patriotism and valour in front of our eyes. To invest in the various National Savings Schemes to support these steadfast souls was the least we could do. Surely, we could all remember those stirring words of Prime Minister Churchill? 'Never in the field of human conflict was so much owed by so many to so few.' Words that applied to the pilots in the Battle of Britain were sentiments we could echo towards all the service personnel who had passed by us on that day. As a town, Bedford had grown from a small settlement of some 2,000 people, doubling in size by the late 18th century. By the time Queen Victoria came to the throne there were still only 9,178 living within its boundaries. Within a hundred years this had exploded sevenfold. It seemed that all those tens of thousands of Bedfordians were out on High Street that day.

As part of the opening ceremony of War Weapons Week, the Tetrarch light tank rolls on its caterpillar tracks past The Embankment. The River Great Ouse flows to the left of the photograph. Guns and warfare have always fascinated little boys. These lads are no exception. Excited, happy faces race along the road beside the armoured vehicle. Boy racers on their bikes act as outriders. It is amusing to modern generations to see such hulking youths sporting school caps. We thought nothing of it then. They were part of the compulsory uniform. Trouble was in store if you were found without it. One headmaster used to fine his pupils a tanner for failing to conform to the rule. No-one knows what the 'school funds' were into which the money was supposed to find its way.

We had our suspicions. This wasn't in Bedford, of course! The happy students would have had a more serious look on their faces if only they had stopped to think. The guns and war games they mimicked on their playground were sources of horror, not fun. Thankfully, peace would come before they would have to march off and face the bullets for real. The tank had only been around as a war machine since 1916, when used on the Somme. The very first ones were no more than modified tractors. They became important to the surge to victory in the Battle of Cambrai, in 1917, when 474 tanks broke through the German lines. They got their name from being moved in secret to the front lines boxed in crates marked 'tanks' as a security measure.

Below: The British have always been good at fund raising. At different times it would be the church roof that needed repair and along we would go to the fete and win some vinegar posing as elderflower wine on the tombola, but we had contributed. On another day we went into the school hall and bought a moth-eaten pencil case our own little Lucy had made. We were out of pocket, but she was pleased and a new set of PE mats would soon be on the way to the gym. The Government recognised this habit of giving to worthwhile causes that existed in the heart of every true Brit. Throughout the war, appeal after appeal would be made. This one was being made in the first week of February 1941. War Weapons Week had come to town. Up and down the country, towns held their own special weeks to support the latest national drive. Britain had entered the war poorly prepared for hostilities with a reborn and rearmed enemy. There had been too many Chamberlains, naively believing Hitler's promises, and not enough Churchills, mistrusting the dictator's every word. After 18 months of warfare on several fronts, the country's weapon reserves were being stretched. The money to restore them was low as budgets in the late 1930s had not put enough into the defence coffers. So, the people were asked to dig deep. The thermometer on EP Rose and Son's department store, promising to give 'Hitler a knock-out', shows how the appeal was doing.

Bottom: Viewing this march along The Embankment, Rothsay Road, you might be forgiven for thinking that this was a display for the benefit of the Royal Navy. The parade is passing close by the War Memorial which commemorates those who fell in both World Wars. A sickening thought is that the name of one of those heading towards Russell Park may now be engraved upon that very Memorial. The long line of 'Jack Tars' has left the Town Bridge, passed the Swan Hotel and is moving past the attractive and well-kept Embankment Gardens that give us such pleasure on a quiet evening's riverside stroll, to-day. This march in June 1943 was no pleasant ramble by the Great Ouse. It was part of the 'Wings for Victory' campaign. All branches of the armed forces lent their support, although the campaign title suggested that it would be the RAF that would benefit. This was not necessarily so. The drive to encourage the population to invest in National Savings would reap money for the general war reserves. It was good advertising by the nation's leaders to make us focus upon one particular aspect. In that way, we could identify better with the appeal. The help that Bedford gave was enormous. Just witness the huge crowds that covered the length of the leafy Embankment. With crowds standing four and five deep on the pavements, many children climbed on walls to get a better view of sailors who were not much older than they were.

Above: The 'Wings for Victory' campaign was in full swing on 15 June 1943. Parades and rallies were held to inspire Britons to contribute funds and materials to the common goal of defeating 'the Hun'. It was a time of jingoistic slogans and much tub-thumping. The war had been going on for nearly four years and there was a danger that people were settling in to a mood of acceptance that this was a normal way of life. The Government had to remind us, especially in the smaller or more rural towns, that the fight for freedom was still in the balance. The enemy was no longer sweeping all before him, but the battle was far from won. Each town set a target as part of the National Savings Campaign. So good were the organisers at rekindling the national fervour that each figure set was nearly always achieved. Aircrew took time off to publicise the appeal and we turned out in force to restate our support. The float is approaching the Embankment corner of High Street. Behind the RAF badge was the birthplace of the author, William Hale White (Mark Rutherford), who was born here in 1831. Far left was the Belfast Linen Warehouse. JA Hague and Son provided sports clothing for the budding Len Huttons and Tom Finneys of the day. Murkett Brothers did business in the motor trade from this prime site for many years, now the site of Swan Court.

Above right: We were encouraged to dig for victory in one Government drive during the war. Every back garden and flower bed became a mini allotment as cabbages and lettuces fought for space among the lines of spuds and peas. In February 1941 we were being encouraged to do a different form of digging. It could have been christened 'Dig deep for victory'. It was actually called War Weapons Week. Pictures and posters on hoardings and handbills flyposted on walls or on church and public notice boards all carried the same message, just expressed in different words. Trouser pocket linings were turned out and purses emptied. Even the back of the armchair was searched for any odd threepenny bit or farthing, even, that could be contributed. Every penny was another nail in the Nazi coffin. Running in parallel were such schemes as War Bonds and National Savings Certificates. We lent money through these to the Government as a form of investment. In this way, greater sums of cash were released to manufacture and buy more munitions to give our armed forces the wherewithal to finish the job. Truth to tell, those investments yielded the lender very little. Perhaps the best return was that the defeat of fascism was the finest dividend we could have got. Was the lady looking at the display inspired enough by the slogans to contribute her fur stole to the cause? Only she could tell us, but she may be long gone by now.

Hotels, business premises and private houses were all damaged by Goering's pride and joy, his Luftwaffe planes. Whilst workmen busied themselves in picking through the debris, the men in suits had their work to do. Someone's tragedy is another's main chance. Was there salvage to be gleaned from here? Is this an opportunity to redevelop the site more profitably? Could the insurance company reduce liability or the insured jack up the loss? Surely not. Bedford businessmen would never have entertained such mercenary thoughts. Those wielding shovels knew what they had to do. What remained of the once proud Assembly Rooms in Midland Road had to be made safe. They could not take the chance of the rest of the building coming crashing to the ground on top of some poor passer-by. First of all, remove what debris, bricks and rubble they safely could. The rest of the shell could then be temporarily shored up until the owners had made up their minds about the future. Then the final death throes of the Assembly Rooms could be completed as it was brought fully to the ground. The same scenario was happening in other streets in other towns across the country. It was only after Bedford had been hit that this was fully realised by its residents. Until then, the Blitz belonged to the cities. It was seen on he newsreels, but not felt. After this night, we would share the same emotions of frustration and anger felt by those who had suffered before us.

Above: Thursday, 23 July 1942 dawned like any other. The war had run nearly half its course, though we did not, of course, know that at the time. What we did know was that the tide was beginning to turn, albeit slowly, against the Axis powers. The USA had routed the Japanese navy at Midway, the Nazis were stretched on the Russian front and Rommel would soon run up against Montgomery at El Alamein. However, at home, we were still hearing of bombing raids by the Luftwaffe on our major cities. If Bedford townspeople had thought that they were far enough away from the large centres of industry to be safe, they were in for a rude awakening. A stray German bomber aimed a stick of bombs at the station but missed. Nobody was hurt. Whether the noise came from a Junkers 88 or a Dornier 17, it did not matter. The result was the same - destruction. The days after the raid that destroyed part of Midland Road and the surrounding area saw people coming to visit, just to see the damage at first hand. With petrol in short supply, hundreds came down the approach from Midland Road station with their pushbikes, stopping off to get a first hand look at the havoc the bombs had wrought. Why does misfortune make good viewing? It happens now on the motorway when drivers 'rubberneck' an accident.

Above right: The search and rescue services of the civil defence movement had to tread carefully. Under this pile of rubble, twisted spars and splintered timbers there might be an unexploded bomb waiting to start ticking away once more. Despite the dangers, there was a job to be done. There might still be people trapped under here. Delay could prove fatal. These brave Bedford souls gave only a passing thought to their own safety as they strove to help others in need. It was not just the menfolk who risked life and limb. Women worked at their shoulders, sharing the same hardships and dangers. This was not a time of women's rights and equal opportunity. This was a time of necessity when chauvinism was relegated in the cause of providing help. There were the Bevin boys who went down the pits to bring up the coal for our industries. Less well known were the Bevin girls. They responded to the Labour minister's call to help the war effort. He recognised that those who volunteered for war work came with a more positive attitude than those who were conscripted. No-one turned a hair to see a woman getting her hands dirty, pulling at the bricks and joists alongside the men. After all, the bombs did not discriminate between the sexes. They blew you to kingdom come just the same.

Below: It is too difficult to ride a bike in Prebend Street in those first few days after the bombing raid on the town. Potholes in the road, shards of glass, bricks and roof tiles are everywhere. If you didn't get a puncture, you would fall off if you rode over one of the pieces of debris that littered the route. Even the wagon was chancing its arm or its shock absorbers. Little groups of people clustered to talk about the shock of the rain of death that fell from above. This was an English sky. How dare those Germans pollute it with their weapons of mass destruction. The gent on the right might be more sensible if he unfurled his brolly. There was still a chance of the odd slate or two slipping from the roof and doing to him what the Luftwaffe had failed to do. In Midland Raod, the Assembly Rooms lay in ruins and the theatre was scarred and badly damaged. Some people said that Bedford was lucky. The Blitz on London began in the autumn of 1940. It continued as a nightly barrage for two months, only abating for raids to take place on Coventry, Manchester, Birmingham, Sheffield and Glasgow. The Luftwaffe soon returned to the capital and by March 1941, over 20,000 Londoners had died. In 1942 the 'Baedeker' attacks on the historic cities of York, Norwich, Bath and Exeter began. Although our town escaped lightly, by comparison, it counted little if it was your house that had been flattened or your wife who was blown to pieces.

Bottom: They may not have been able to shoulder a rifle and join in the fight against Hitler's war machine, but the people of Bedford were all prepared to do their bit for King and country. In 1940 a massive salvage drive was organised, and the cry of 'Any old iron' took on a new meaning as hundreds of thousands responded to the appeal. They sacrificed their iron bedsteads, tin baths, iron railings and aluminium saucepans by the thousand and sent them off to the scrapyards to be turned into Spitfires and Hurricanes. The sacrifices during World War II were many and varied, from this wholesale donation of scrap metal to collections of clothing, bedding, furniture and toys, which went via organisations such as the WVS to families who had lost everything in bombing raids.

Knowledge alone is not enough

Bedford College which stands proudly above the banks of the Great Ouse River was for decades an unreachable dream. Several generations of Bedfordians were regaled, by both the Bedford Chronicle and the Bedford Times, with details of proposals, costs and the delays which prevented the provision of a permanent home for Further Education in Bedford. Reports of council meetings on the matter were every bit as frequent as the town's leaders considered the pros and cons of each site, a process which lasted some sixty years.

It is not that Bedford lacked facilities for Further Education for, as Queen Victoria's great reign drew to an end, the Bedford Technical Institute provided the educational and training facilities normal to all industrial towns. Like other such institutes in their early days the BTI utilised existing educational institutions, namely Bedford School and Bedford Modern School, for its evening classes. Unlike fellow students in sister industrial towns Bedfordians continued to make do for some fifty years.

FUTURE OF BEDFORD MODERN SCHOOL

A STATEMENT FROM THE SCHOOL MAGAZINE

The first item in the very interesting current issue of *The Eagle* (the journal of the Bedford Modern School) is headed " The School and the future " and reads as follows:—

The possibility of the School's leaving its present site and being rebuilt elsewhere has received so much publicity that we have been asked by Old Boys to make a statement of the issues involved, and to trace the main outlines of the discussions, which have as yet not reached any final decision.

(a) At the Centenary Dinner in 1933 the late Sir Maurice Craig referred to the re-building of the School as inevitable.

(b) For some years there has been a general feeling that the present buildings are quite inadequate for the educational requirements of a school of over six hundred boys. Accommodation is so cramping that the small hall of the old Victory Café, opposite the Harper Street gates, has, since September 1936, been rented as an additional classroom. There are several other serious limitations of space, as for example the inadequacy of the gymnasium to meet the demands of modern physical education, the lack of suitable changing-room accommodation, and the absence of a general library and reading-room apart from the Reference Library.

was a two term year running from September to March with a one month break at Christmas, ranged between half a crown (2/6d, one eighth of a pound or 12.5p) to 12/6d per session dependent on age and course taken. These included all commercial subjects and three foreign languages while the engineering classes, vital to the local economy, covered in addition not only plumbing and decorating but the skills of telegraphy and telephoning. Progressive offices were then installing telephones to replace the messengers who ran around the town and shipping companies were seeking well trained Radio Telegraphists to man ships' Wireless 'shacks'. The GPO (General Post Office) employed telegraph operators, to send and receive the hand delivered telegrams used for urgent messages, for another thirty years.

The Art Department offered courses in Architecture and Surveying, Cabinet Making and Carving (both wood and stone), Jewellery and Metal Work and, a sign of the times, courses in the still mysterious trade of Photography. The BTI ran all these in borrowed buildings designed

Bedford College Archives contain numbers of the annual brochures produced by the BTI to attract students to its courses. That for the session of 1923/1924 outlines rules and standards some of which modern students might regard askance. Methods of study were stipulated while no certificates would be granted to any student failing to achieve 75% attendance, 40% marks and a good report. Details of homework expectations were laid down, as were those of examinations to be taken and a no nonsense attitude to discipline. For all that the 1920s were known as the 'Roaring Twenties', when 'Flappers' demonstrated a new feminine independence, young ladies normally obeyed their parent's, mentor's and employer's directions. The BTI was no exception, and yet, in informing prospective students of the existence of a ladies lavatory in Bedford Modern College, it accepted the importance of educated females to the Bedford economy.

Matriculation classes cost from one to two guineas (£1-1s-0d or £1.05p to a guinea). The costs, for what

Top: The announcement to the students of the College's expansion plans.
Right: The building of the new College.

for school use, still having no real facilities of its own. People then accepted such limitations as part of life and simply got on with the job of improving their prospects with the tools available at the time. Generations of dedicated instructors, aided by spirited co-operation from the two schools and the administrative staff of the town's Education Committee's, not to mention eager students, made it work. An attitude which enabled the post-war

Mander College to operate successfully from its temporary buildings on the edge of a riverside building site. The courses run in the first year of the second world war were so expanded with additional subjects that classes were held in the Central School in addition to the existing site.

Above: *A view of the College as seen in the early 1960s.*

For all that Bedfordians lacked a college building of their own the town was graced by two Teacher Training establishments. The 'doyenne' of Higher Education in Bedford was undoubtedly Bedford Froebelian Institute, established in The Crescent since 1880.

Public education, as established by law in the early 1870s, was a regimented affair of learning by rote in huge classes kept in order by liberal use of the cane. More modern methods brought enjoyment and individuality into schools by encouraging youngsters to think and to relate education to the outside world in a manner now regarded as normal.

The second institution of Higher Education in the town was the Bedford Physical Training College where gym teachers were trained between 1903 and 1993. Generations of girls who have adored or loathed games with equal passion can thank the well trained alumni of Bedford PTC for introducing them to the pleasures, or hardships, of the games field. Such capable teachers have often been derided as 'Jolly hockey-sticks' types but their tradition of caring enthusiasm continues in the sports scientists of today who, between 1976-1993,

were trained under the banner of Bedford College of Higher Education. Both of these famous ladies' colleges later liaised socially with the male students of nearby Silsoe College of Agricultural Engineering and Shuttleworth College of Agriculture, eight miles to the east.

Following the end of World War II the North Bedfordshire College of Further Education, run by Bedfordshire County Council Education Committee, assumed the mantle of the fifty year old Bedford Technical Institute. The prospectus for 1948-1949 shows the North Bedfordshire College of Further Education located between Cauldwell Street and St Mary's Embankment as the current home of Mander College. In July 1947 builders started constructing temporary concrete buildings to be ready by January 1949, which were in use for over a decade until replaced by the tall riverside tower opened, on the 19th

Above: The teaching staff in the 1950s with the College in the background.
Right: *A presentation by College governors in the 1950s.*

June 1959, by The Rt. Hon. 'RAB' Butler, Secretary of State for Home Affairs. Although enjoying its first taste of a new home the expanded college still rented accommodation from the Bedford schools known to several generations of FE students. Practical courses followed local custom in catering for the engineering, scientific and commercial needs of North Bedfordshire. More esoteric classes existed in Matriculation and Foreign Languages, Art and Social Studies while Non-vocational courses offered a variety of leisure time subjects.

The Autumn 1950 issue of 'The Student' Magazine contained a paragraph from a 16 year old student contemplating her first holiday without her family but with a 17 year old girl friend. Such daring young ladies, wearing daringly short shorts, were a common and attractive sight in the Youth Hostels of the period, even so it was then a big step towards adulthood. Another element of modern life was the provision of car parking spaces for students. Regulations on smoking and behaviour were little changed from earlier days as colleges continued to act firmly 'in loco parentis' until the 'Swinging Sixties' combined with plentiful youth employment in eroding family life. Fees had risen to between £15 and £21 per year for day students at a time when residential colleges, like public schools, were charging from £300 to £500 pa, all in.

Mander College was named after Sir Frederick Mander, Chairman of Bedfordshire County Council at the time

that the dream became reality. The tall tower which housed the college, although likened by some critics to the 'blunt end of a tanker', was typical of its period's best architectural design. The long sides of continuous windows gave light to every room while the two ends, containing stairs and toilets, were multi-hued to enliven the scene. The entrance is protected by an overhanging concrete porch, with no visible means of support, which leads into the spacious and airy Entrance Hall from which wide, shallow stairs lead to the broad Mezzanine Gallery. This first block was erected for a cost of £282,510, rather more than double the estimates submitted twenty years earlier, plus another £4,085 for external works.

The well equipped Mander College provided courses covering all aspects of Further and Higher Education from GCEs to HNCs. City and Guilds syllabuses vied with the Royal Society of Arts in offering employable qualifications. Students could work for diplomas, be examined by the Union of Educational Institutes and take external degree courses set by the major universities. Classes in music and drama were an important part of the Bedford cultural scene as were non-vocational classes for part time students. There were even proposals afoot to make Mander College the National Centre for both aero technology and the locally based brick and heavy clay technologies as well as the Regional Centre for the gas

Above: *Presentation of books to Mander College Library by Mr Harry Manning - October 1963.*

industry and allied crafts. This too reflected the importance of the links between the Mander College and Bedford's unique local industries.

Courses for local people included 'Farmers and Growers Evenings on VAT Returns' when speakers endeavoured to unravel the complexities of a tax system operated by the taxpayer. In 1972 Mander students rose in anger because they were expected to work on the day of celebration of the Queen's Silver Wedding when the other colleges enjoyed a day's holiday. Mrs Barbara Castle MP led a Labour Party Rally at Mander attended by students in the height of 'Flower Power' fashion of flared trousers and flowing locks. By contrast the Student Governor of the same year was photographed neatly clad in suit and tie as befitted the importance of his role.

Other events which made local headlines were a concert by Cy Grant, a popular TV guitarist, and the Christmas Tea Party, given by students, for thirty local children. Shirley Williams, MP forecast major ventures in education when guest of honour at the 1974 Prize Giving; perhaps she knew of the controversial merger planned for Bedford's three colleges. The new Haylage silo at Mander College Farm, Silsoe took the grass from twenty two and a half acres (around nine hectares) to provide winter fodder, 180 days worth, for the college herd of eighty-five dairy cattle. This splendid tower saved the farm enterprise £3,000 in bought-in supplements in that winter alone!

Some thirteen years after the opening of Mander College it was combined with the two teacher training institutions into one of those split-site colleges popular at the time. The trio was then renamed the Bedford College of Higher Education, each part continuing with its time honoured and separate task in its own buildings. The merger, designed to save money on behalf of local ratepayers, had cost an extra £38,000, sufficient to pay the salaries of half a dozen teachers. The three campuses provided residential places for six hundred of the two thousand or so students. The Physical Training College enjoyed an enviable international reputation while the Teacher Training College, then relocated in Polhill Road, was up to the minute in running industrial management and teacher training

Below: *Student brickwork, Kempston.*
Bottom: *Aerospace Engineering facility.*

courses side by side to break down old barriers between academics and businesses. Such good relationships survived the protest made by local firms whose employees on part-time courses were automatically enrolled in the Students Union at the employers' expense.

The amalgamated colleges co-existed for seventeen years providing trade oriented training alongside teacher training and non-vocational classes. Two success stories, which proved that 'sec-mod' pupils could make the grade in Higher Education, were of students Mario Dimonace, who worked part time in an ice-cream van, and Sikder Sangherra, both of whom made their way, in 1977, into Medical School. Student events included the college's famous fund raising Rag Week and a protest to the College's former guest of honour, Mrs Shirley Williams. As that capable lady had survived worse, (including being burned in effigy when Minister of Transport), she, the College and the students all got on with life.

Dennis Howell, MP, the first Minister of Sport, opened the handsomely appointed new Sports Hall, which at £289,000 had cost as much as the main block, at the end of the year.

The daring students taking Seamanship and Advanced Navigation proved that even inlanders have salt in their veins by hiring a £100,000 yacht for a cross Channel

voyage enlivened by 50mph gales! The campus also played an important part in local cultural life by inviting famous musicians to participate in the regular 'Music at Mander' musical evenings. Amongst the Maestros who enhanced the Bedford cultural scene were John Ogden, the concert pianist, and Evelyn Barbirolli, the oboeist. On a different scale were the more frequent musical feasts for which tickets cost 30-50p and joint events in which local amateurs - including the author of this piece who, as a student, sang at the Bedford Festival in the Repertory Theatre.

Above: *The College library.*
Top: *A typical class.*

After thirteen years of academic marriage the pressure on facilities had grown through constant development to such a stage that finding space for every activity was a major problem. In 1992 FE Colleges became independent of Local Education Authorities. The decision was made to concentrate the Further Education elements at Cauldwell Street to continue the tradition started by the old Technical Institute. Bedford College became an FE Corporation running in addition Enterprise House at Queen's Park and the Motor Vehicle Training and Construction Centres in Kempston.

The rather different needs of the Higher Education departments were to be housed on a site of their own. In 1994 the Higher Education activity was separated to form the new de Monfort University.

Throughout its fascinating history of development and 'house hunting' for a permanent home what is now a noble flagship of Further Education has served the students and town of Bedford well. Many who read this will have personal or family links with the college which has shaped the destinies and fostered the careers of Bedfordians. Others will have had the satisfaction of enriching their leisure time either by learning anew half forgotten arts and skills or branching out into new, often profitable, fields. All those who dreamed of and worked for the cause of Further Education in Bedford can look at Bedford College with pride and satisfaction in the achievements of all involved as this great institution nears the One Hundredth Anniversary of Further Education in Bedford.

Left and below: *The College today.*

Events & occasions

Below: Somewhere in every house in the land in the 1950s and 1960s you could still dig out that Coronation mug. Given out at schools and Sunday schools across the nation, they were kept as a symbol of that great day when our Queen was crowned. They might be chipped and cracked. They might be used to hold pens and pencils. They might even be used to drink tea from, but they would not be thrown away. Whenever it was time for a clear out don't you dare chuck away my Coronation mug. If the handle fell off, a spot of glue soon sorted that out. The little tots in the photograph would treasure the memento of a day when we celebrated as never before, at least since VE and VJ days. It had been eight long years of austerity. Few sweets, little chocolate and what was that curved, yellow fruit we had heard about? Here was something special coming to us for free. The face of the young Queen painted on the mug looked out at us from its pride of place on the mantelpiece above the fire. It made a good set with the Coronation crown, the five shilling piece in its little display case. Posh schools gave those out as well. The rest of us had to buy them from the post office. It was worth it. We knew we were part of a historic occasion. We were unlikely to see its like this side of the year 2000.

Right: Midland Road curves eastward towards Silver Street and the High Street beyond. On the left, Woolworth's and Sainsbury's stand close to the attractive, rounded dome of Marks and Spencer. It is a bright, sunny day and hopes are high for the great day to-morrow. The awnings are all pulled down to shelter the shop goods from the strong sunlight. Faded clothes and over-ripe produce won't sell. It may be the eve of a momentous occasion, but the shopkeeper was not going to let sentiment take over from common sense. Whilst council workmen and shop assistants worked overhead putting up the decorations and streamers, life went on normally underneath. It was Monday, after all. The shopping basket and larder had to be topped up from the weekend. Extra provisions were needed to help the street parties and celebrations go with a swing. The odd bottle of aspirin might come in handy, too, if some of the gaiety was taken to excess. Some foodstuffs were still in short supply, but the ration book would take a hammering to-day. The British knew how to party. In the meantime, the good old bobby was keeping a watchful eye on the rickety platform and shepherding vehicles round it. The last thing he wanted to see was the chaps on top of the planking having to swing in mid air like some trapeze artist if their tower was swept away from under them.

The banner to Elizabeth Regina hangs nobly near the edge of St Paul's Square as High Street leads away to the north. The use of the royal initials has been quite economical during the 20th century. VR, ER and GR are all we have needed. Presumably, we will need CR in the new millennium, but not just yet, we hope. No thoughts of future Kings distracted Bedford people at the time of this photograph. After all, little Charles was a mere toddler of four and his mother a youthful 27. The cars parked on the market square would have to find new resting places when it became a pedestrian only spot. A merchant guild had been set up in medieval times in order to control and regulate the market and trade generally. Their problems would

have included monitoring the flow of carts piled with farm produce. The idea that people needed to be carried in horseless carriages and demand places to leave them for hours on end is a feature of the 20th century. As a new millennium dawns, planners are taking us back to the days of walking around towns by banishing the car to more isolated spots. High Street was the birthplace of William H White, who wrote under the name of Mark Rutherford. The 19th century author and Admiralty civil servant was concerned with religious problems and ordeals of the heart. No such troubles for our Queen on this day. She had the Archbishop of Canterbury and Prince Philip to look after her spiritual and temporal needs.

Above: On the corner of Silver Street the streamers are still being hauled into place. It may be midnight, but the final touches have to be in place for to-morrow. It is hardly something that you can be late with! Fancy having to tell your grandchildren that you did not finish the Coronation decorations on time. The foreman would not have been likely to accept an excuse or a suggestion that they could be finished in the morning. By then the streets would start to fill with the new monarch's subjects, all keen to wave the flag for Britain. It was no good saying that the streamers would keep until next time. That was likely to be in the next century, There was nothing else for it. Roll up your sleeves, lads, and fix that hook to the corner of EP Rose's store. It is to be hoped that these workmen had a lookout on duty around the corner. The last thing they would want is for some early reveller to come whizzing around the corner in his Austin Seven and bowl the lot of them over.

Top: Bedford grew up around a ford across the River Great Ouse. The Anglo-Saxon sovereign Edward the Elder recaptured it from the Danes in the year 914. The community became the shire capital because of its commanding position. It received its first surviving charter from King Henry II in 1166. High Street, running down from the crossroads at Mill Street and Silver Street towards The Town Bridge, became the main shopping centre. Although modern developments around the pedestrianised areas and the opening of the Harpur Centre mall have shifted trade, at the time of the Coronation it still held a powerful position. On the left, the Red Lion was a popular watering hole for those wishing to toast the new Head of the Commonwealth. It was a good excuse for another pint to insist on showing your loyalty to the crown by proposing another round in honour of Her Majesty. The missus would forgive you just this once, though she raised her eyes to heaven as though to say 'Does he really need an excuse to bend his arm, yet again?' Drinking places may have changed along this street as the years have passed. The modern toper is supposed to enjoy supping in places with quaint names, like the Hobgoblin. The seasoned tippler is more interested in the brew's quality than some effete title.

What a day that was. We can't wait to get back to work to talk about it. Cars are clogging up High Street once again as things return to normal. There won't be much done in the typing pool to-day. All the talk will be of the glamour of the young Queen and the street parties that were held in every town and village across the county. From Biggleswade to Flitwick old and young rejoiced together. Orangeade flowed almost as much as the ale. There was not a house that did not have a flag hanging out of a bedroom window. There might be a few thick heads as one or two of us celebrated a little too keenly the night before. High above Bedford's main shopping street the streamers

and bunting will stay for another few days. Eventually, the council workmen will come to remove them. The last time we rejoiced so merrily was at the end of the war. Who can say when the next big do will come? Anyone good at maths could have answered that question. It would come in 1977, when the Silver Jubilee would conjure up similar scenes. The flags and streamers might be new, but there would be no change in the patriotic fervour as chairs and tables appeared in the streets once more. If only we could share that sense of national togetherness more often. Someone should bottle it and sell it to us as a tonic for life's everyday ills.

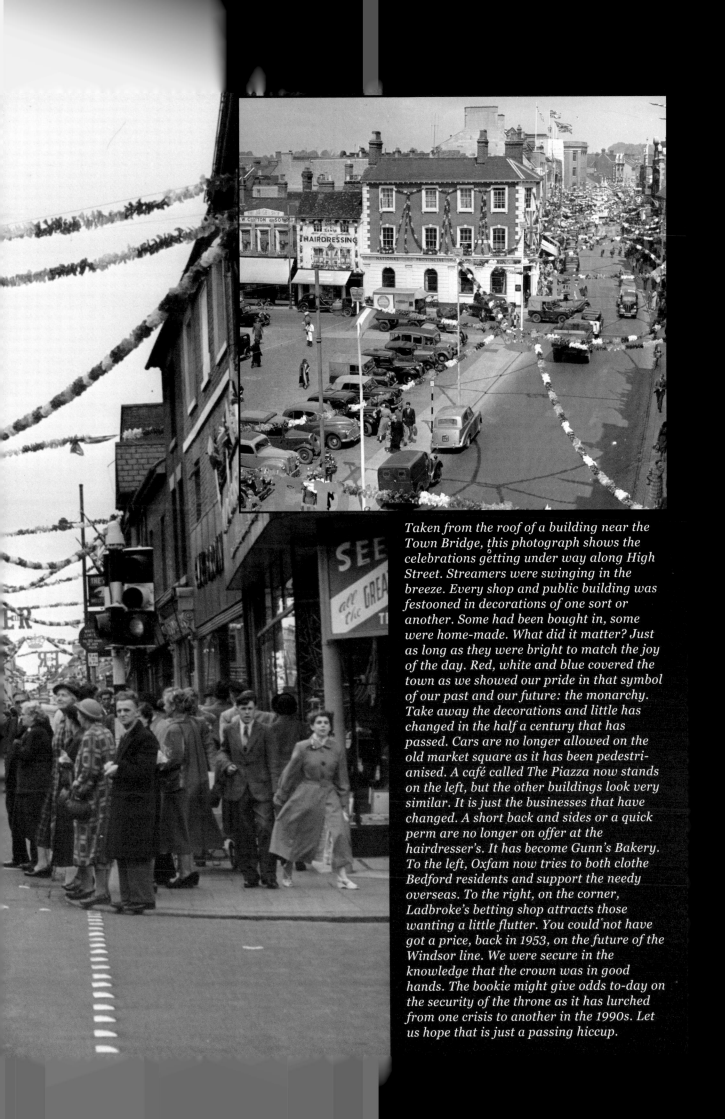

Taken from the roof of a building near the Town Bridge, this photograph shows the celebrations getting under way along High Street. Streamers were swinging in the breeze. Every shop and public building was festooned in decorations of one sort or another. Some had been bought in, some were home-made. What did it matter? Just as long as they were bright to match the joy of the day. Red, white and blue covered the town as we showed our pride in that symbol of our past and our future: the monarchy. Take away the decorations and little has changed in the half a century that has passed. Cars are no longer allowed on the old market square as it has been pedestrianised. A café called The Piazza now stands on the left, but the other buildings look very similar. It is just the businesses that have changed. A short back and sides or a quick perm are no longer on offer at the hairdresser's. It has become Gunn's Bakery. To the left, Oxfam now tries to both clothe Bedford residents and support the needy overseas. To the right, on the corner, Ladbroke's betting shop attracts those wanting a little flutter. You could not have got a price, back in 1953, on the future of the Windsor line. We were secure in the knowledge that the crown was in good hands. The bookie might give odds to-day on the security of the throne as it has lurched from one crisis to another in the 1990s. Let us hope that is just a passing hiccup.

Above: For the first time in their lives, this group of senior citizens gathered around the marvel of the modern techno-logical age in 1953. The tiny black and white pictures flickered on the small screen of the huge box on the table in front of them. They were attracted like moths to the flame, hypnotised by what was happening in front of them. They had lived through the age of radio and the telephone. These were wonders enough, but you had to use your imagination to conjure an image to go with the sound. Now there was no need to think. The scene was developing, as Arthur Askey might have put it, 'before your very eyes'. Is it any surprise that later generations would dump their children in front of the 'goggle box' rather than bother to entertain them by playing or reading? Two events can be blamed for popular-ising the TV set. The first was the dramatic FA Cup Final in May. Stanley (later Sir Stanley) Matthews won his medal at the ripe old age of 38 in a game that finished 4-3 to Blackpool. Neighbours gathered around a street's single set and vowed to watch the next great event together. It was to come the following month. In sitting rooms and rest rooms across Britain the Queen's subjects had a bird's-eye view of royalty that had only been glimpsed from the pavement when she whizzed by on an official visit. These old people felt as though they were in Westminster Abbey with her.

Above right: Switch on the set. Let the valves warm up and, eventually, the little screen came to life. It hummed and crackled, but it was a real picture of events happening now. This was a time of adjusting the vertical and horizontal holds as picture frames wandered up, down and across the screen. The reception might be snowy, but who cared? Pathé News could bring us the pictures a few days later at the cinema, but this was live. To make it the perfect day, there was the fruity, sober voice of Richard Dimbleby to describe the scene for us. How well he brought the impor-

tance and historical significance of the occasion into our homes. The old folk had never seen anything to rival this day, nor would they again. Elizabeth had been Queen for over a year, since the death of her father George VI, in 1952. Preparations had been painstaking, but the success of the ceremony in being the first people's Coronation made it worthwhile. Dr Fisher, the Archbishop of Canterbury, conducted the service. Afterwards, the newly crowned monarch rode in the Golden Coronation Coach to Buckingham Palace. We could follow every move, thanks to good old Auntie, 'the Beeb'. Who can forget that special sight of Queen Salote, a huge and beaming figure, waving vigorously as her open carriage filled with rainwater. Bowler hats disappeared into the air when Queen Elizabeth II appeared on the balcony at the Palace. Hundreds of thousands finished the day on Victoria Embankment, watching fireworks whoosh skywards. By then these happy viewers were in the land of Nod, privileged to have shared in the day.

Ration coupons have been jealously hoarded and cashed in to provide goodies for the children's party. Pilgrim's Way, just off Mile Road, was like all others in Britain. There was a celebration to be had and the residents were not going to be denied their fun. Public halls had been taken over for the day. School gym equipment was moved to one side. The church prayer books had been carefully tidied away. All morning the dads had blown up balloons and climbed up ladders to put up the colourful bunting. Union Jacks and Royal Standards hung everywhere. Mums popped little cakes and buns in and out of ovens and Gran helped with the sandwich spread and meat paste. Then it was time for it all to come together. Trestle tables, chairs and benches were dragged into line and the kids sat under their party hats waiting to be given the signal to start scoffing. Children could be patient in June 1953. It is a shame that their offspring have proved less so. Posing for the group picture, not a crumb has been moved, nor will it be until the 'off' is indicated. Then, within 10 minutes, the lot will have disappeared. In the meantime, raise your beakers to salute Queen Elizabeth who is to be crowned to-day.

What a pity. The Queen is being crowned to-day and here we are, on the second day of June, dressed in the height of 1953 fashion in raincoats and sheltering under umbrellas. The tables, benches and chairs have been dragged out onto Fenlake Road, to the south of Bedford, for the street party. Soggy sandwiches and damp cakes have been polished off, along with several gallons of 'pop' poured from proper glass bottles with stoppers. No plastic Pepsi for us, thank you very much. The Union flags flutter limply from the windows of the houses behind. The only ones not worried about the weather are the nippers enjoying their fancy dress party. These little dears will be over 50 by now and, perhaps, have grandchildren of their own to spoil. On that special day, they have had their parade and are now examining the prize and certificate given to the one judged to have the best costume. Is it dad who is looking on proudly? What does it matter. The children were all winners on that day. They were less worried about coming first than their doting parents. Kids enjoyed a party for what it was - a celebration and a bit of fun. It is only the adults who are into competition, using their children as a source of reflected glory. Why else did Mrs Higgins use three months' worth of clothing coupons to make Bessie's ballerina outfit? Serves her right that the little monster was sick all down it and never even made the parade.

Right: The Prime Minister, Harold Macmillan, was fulfilling a series of speaking engagements in July 1957. In both Bradford and Bedford he delivered the same message, 'Some of our people have never had it so good'. He was speaking from a podium on the football ground of Bedford Town AFC. The rally had been organised by several Bedfordshire Conservative Associations, including the Luton branch of the party. Sir John Howard was the chairman of the organising committee. Sir Harold Wernher introduced the PM to a cheering crowd. He mentioned the troubles in Cyprus, where EOKA terrorists, led by General Grivas and politically supported by Archbishop Makarios, were creating problems for Britain. Macmillan rose to the challenge and banished negative thoughts. He told his audience to go around the country and see a state of prosperity as there had never been in his lifetime. The crowd was already buoyed by the overnight news that the runner, Derek Ibbotson, had smashed the world mile record. How it cheered the man not best known for inspirational words. Macmillan found it difficult to motivate the masses. He hated television broadcasts, coming over as a stilted and uncertain performer. But, he had the bit between his teeth that day. One of politics' great mis-quoted catch-phrases had been born. He was right. Compared with the austere days of the early 50s, the life we were having was good. Jobs were a-plenty and a new dawn was well and truly over the horizon.

Below: After delivering his so-called 'You've never had it so good' address, Mr Macmillan mingled with the rank and file of the Tory party faithful. For a man who represented the generally right wing views of middle England, he was still capable of springing surprises. He went to South Africa in February 1960 and told the Parliament in Capetown that there was a 'Wind of change blowing through this continent'. He was referring to the country's apartheid laws and the need to look forward to a time when the black African had a share in the running of the country. The remarks horrified Prime Minister Verwoerd and his followers. The Macmillan speech was 30 years ahead of its time, for it was not until 1994 that Nelson Mandela became the South African president. At home, Macmillan was able to lead the Tory Government in passing several bills that provided social benefit for the general public. In doing so he gained the support of former Labour voters. As an Oxford graduate and veteran of combat in World War I, he was already guaranteed the approval of Conservatives. Having replaced Anthony Eden as Prime Minister at the beginning of 1957, he won the 1959 election at a canter. His ability to unite the country led his main opponent, Hugh Gaitskell, to remark, 'The class war is now obsolete.' Cartoonist 'Vicky' drew him as 'Supermac', flying through the air on his way to solve the world's problems. He resigned in 1963, because of ill health. He died in 1986, aged 92.

The late lamented Granada was very important in Bedford's history, although no-one was too bothered what was showing in June 1966. On this day, who was inside the limousine sweeping from St Peter's Street into The Broadway at the top end of the High Street was more to the point. The statue of John Bunyan, with his flowing locks, his book clasped in his hands and billowing cape stands just off camera to the left. He, like the rest of us, was waiting to greet a special visitor. The royal standard fluttering from the car's roof gives a clue to the identity of the main passenger. It is Queen Elizabeth, the Queen Mother. Then a young 65, she was far from living the life of a pensioner. For years she has been known with affection as the Queen Mum. But, she has always been hardworking, fulfilling a heavy calendar of royal engagements. This day she has come to preside at the ceremony of laying up the old colours of the Fifth Battalion of the Bedfordshire and Hertfordshire Regiment (TA). Even in the blasé swinging sixties, a royal visit was still a special occasion to wave little flags and let HRH know that we loved her dearly. The street corner was packed with well-wishers keen to display their patriotism. The flags would come in handy at the end of the next month. They would be waved in celebration as England's soccer team lifted the World Cup.

Crowds packed the roads from the Town Bridge to St Paul's Square just to try and catch a glimpse of the former Elizabeth Bowes-Lyon. Dressed in her usual attractive pastel shades, topped with a favourite fluffy hat, the widow of the former King George VI, moved across St Paul's Square with that elegance of royalty. War medals and dress uniforms show the importance of the occasion to the Fifth Battalion of the Bedfordshire and Hertfordshires. The crowd to the left, in front of the Shire Hall, stands calmly without the need for crush barriers to keep it back. Bedford people were too polite to indulge in anything so crass. A pleasant sign of the times is the absence of bodyguards. Respect for royalty was still the order of the day in 1966. However, no doubt, in an emergency, the Lord Lieutenant's sword would have made short shrift of anyone attempting to hurt the Queen Mum. She was much too loved for anyone to try. The crowd would have torn such a villain limb from limb, if the blade failed to do the trick. Behind the official party, on their way to the Shire Hall for a reception, are the old and new Town Halls. The front of the former, on the right, houses a statue of William Harpur, with a Latin inscription to 'Gulielmi Harpur'.

The Shire Hall now contains the magistrates' courts and the cells for those waiting to be brought before the 'beak'.

Bottom: It was time to wave goodbye to the Queen Mum. The new dining rooms had been officially opened in the building that had been home to Dame Alice Harpur School since 1938. Situated on Cardington Road, with a fine view of the Great Ouse, the school has enjoyed the benefits of well equipped classrooms and fine open playing spaces. Hockey fields, tennis and netball courts provided these daughters of Bedford with a healthy break from the rigours of trigonometry and Latin grammar. Young ladies played games that were games for young ladies. Why do girls have to play rugby and soccer just to satisfy the politically correct of the 1990s? On the day of our photo the head girl, Margaret Eborall, and the headmistress, Miss H Lawson-Brown, had a time to cherish to their dying day. They and the prefects and monitors took tea with the Queen Mother before she took her leave. At 4.15 she walked across the field to her helicopter and waved a last farewell. Back in Bedford, the Town Clerk, Mr GF Simmonds, could be heard praising his staff and breathing a quiet sigh of relief that the day went smoothly. The girls of the Dame Alice Harpur School were not too concerned about his anxieties. They were happy to wave and shout ecstatically to let their guest know of the pride and pleasure she had brought to them this day. A return to two hours of French homework would be with them soon enough. In the meantime, enjoy the moment. Even the teachers managed a small smile. Now, that did make it a special day.

Right: Little girls in neat uniforms and summer dresses wait for the Queen Mother to arrive. She has finished her duty at the army ceremony in the town centre and is on her way to Dame Alice Harpur School. In June 1966

white ankle socks were part and parcel of a summer uniform. They look like proper girl students. It is a far cry from the tights, jeans and leggings that are the scruffy garb of so many these days. Patiently waiting in ordered rows, the young ladies are ready to greet their royal guest. She is coming to officially open the new dining rooms. The school had a wealth of history behind it. Local man, Sir William Harpur, who went on to become Lord Mayor of London, endowed a charitable and educational trust which established a school in Bedford in 1566. It replaced the school run by the monks of Newnham Priory. Sir William and his wife, Dame Alice were the founders of the Bedford Charity. The Harpur Trust was set up in 1764 to administer the endowment. From 1882 there were two schools each for boys and girls. Both girls' schools were in Bromham Road. In 1892 the High School took over the whole site and the Girls' Modern School (today called Dame Alice Harpur School) moved to St Paul's Square.

On the home front

If this were 1665 and the Great Plague, the cry of 'Bring out your dead' would be appropriate. Fortunately, these barrows are to be used for a different purpose in the summer of 1942. Throughout the war years, appeals for junk and salvage were continuous. Sometimes we were asked to hand over old saucepans, flat irons and garden railings to provide scrap metal, supposedly for the building of new warships and planes. It seemed ironic that the Spitfire overhead might really be a flying frying pan. Not to worry, as long as it did its job. The British, weaned on a diet of jumble sales and white elephant stalls, were past masters (and mistresses) at scavenging. The skill was to serve them well. Wastepaper was the focus of this collection. The aim was to collect a mile of books and

recycle the paper. The drive for paper had begun in 1941. Local councils competed in the national £20,000 wastepaper competition. In November 1941 Bedford collected 19 tons, valued at £83. In December this increased to 51 tons (£244). Bins were erected in St Paul's Square and on St Peter's. Reading was one of the nation's favourite ways of passing time. No television, of course, and every household had a host of books which had been stored away in attics and boxes. It was time to bring them out and put them to use in the war effort. 'Bring out your books and beat the Bosch' was the quaintly spelled message. The leafy road, leading from Bedford Park, is De Parys Avenue. It was named after Robert de Parys who founded St John's Hospital for the aged poor, circa 1200.

Above: In November 1941 a presentation is being made to the Land Army girls for their special service to the county's agriculture. Their contribution was vital during the war years in keeping the food chain moving. Many male farmworkers had volunteered or been called up to serve King and country. Eighty-five women joined the Land Army at the start of the war, the number rising to 1,000 in Bedfordshire by 1944. Women had filled important roles during the Great War and their daughters rallied to the cause with the same patriotic zeal. In the following month all single women between the ages of 20 and 30 would be conscripted. So acute was the war personnel problem that Mr Churchill had to call for this instalment of 'further sacrifice and exertion'. These girls had heard the call before that. Most of them had gladly volunteered to leave home and live in hostels or on the farms just to 'do their bit'. The sight of the knee-length ribbed socks and breeches, topped by the sturdy jumper was to become a common one in the fields and country lanes of rural England. An army marches on its stomach, but it was this army that helped feed it. As the war dragged on, the Coalition Government brought out further legislation. In May 1943 the Minister of Labour , Ernest Bevin, aimed a measure at those women who had been slow to offer their help in defeating the enemy. Part-time war work became compulsory for all women aged between 18 and 45 who did not have domestic responsibilities. These Land Army girls would not have worried.They had recognised their duty years before.

Above right: It is time to take a welcome break at the Bedford Land Army Girls' Club. A new club at Milton Ernest would open in 1942. After yet another day wielding a pitchfork, digging a ditch or mending a fence there is little energy left for anything more strenuous than a darn good read. The latest Agatha Christie whodunit will do nicely as a piece of escapism from the backbreaking ordeals of the day. As well

as locals, many of the girls had come from the big cities to contribute to the war effort. Summertime pictures of them on the top of hayricks might have looked idyllic, but this was late autumn in 1941 and outdoor work was far from glamorous. It was not without its dangers. Apart from injuries caused by machinery and sharp tools, there was always the possibility that a POW might turn nasty. Sometimes prisoners worked alongside the girls. In July 1943 one Italian POW was working in the fields when he escaped, slitting a guard's throat. He used his victim's rifle to fire at one young girl worker. Few tears were shed when he was cornered and killed. As the 1940s went by, additions to the Land Army were made. The sister wing of the Emergency Land Corps was born. Bedfordshire women who had worked all day as housewives, clerks, teachers, shopgirls etc spent their evening and weekend spare time in the fields. They would meet outside the Bedford Corn Exchange to be ferried to work. They would be expected to give a minimum of 48 hours of their time. Anyone achieving 100 hours gained a stripe on her armlet. Better still, she gained the country's thanks.

Below: Care in the community was an important aspect of the work of Bedford's Public Health Department. The WVS (from 1966 WRVS) volunteers had pioneered meals on wheels and home helps in the immediate post-war years. Councils were slow to respond, but with a more socially conscious Labour Party in control after 1945, the government brought pressure to bear on those who were dragging their feet. The Tories continued the programme of social reform, particularly under Macmillan. By June 1959, this elderly couple may have been one of many affected by the new mobility of the workforce. No longer did families live within striking distance of each other. A generation had been lost in the 1939-45 war. The old were often alone and forgotten. In 1948, the first charges for a hot meal were a tanner for a main dish and tuppence for a pudding. Not only did the meal warm the insides of the elderly and the infirm, it was a way of keeping in touch.

The person making the delivery became a friend whose visit was eagerly awaited. Providing help around the house with cleaning or shopping meant that OAPs did not have to retreat to a home and lose their independence. The home help's call was always a good excuse to get out the best china and share in a cup of tea and a good chinwag.

Bottom: Comparing notes and patterns, these members of the Silsoe knitting party all belong to the local branch of the Women's Voluntary Service. Lady Stella Reading founded the organisation as a follow-up to her work in the Personal Service League which helped families affected by the depression years of the early 1930s. While other WVS members were on the front line supporting the rescue and emergency services, these women provided important back up. The casting on, the knitting, purling and the passing over of slip stitches had an effect on the war effort. As the needles clacked across each other, jumpers, socks, cardigans and woolly toys started to take shape. Some of these might go direct to soldiers in need of extra warm clothing. Other finished articles would be sold at fetes, socials and church fairs. The money raised went into the pot of the latest fund raising drive. It might be to provide cash to support the building of a Hurricane, a tank or a submarine. Not that it really mattered. These ladies just wanted to do their bit in helping the war effort. Count them and you can see that this is the Silsoe First 13. Whatever side Adolf put out hadn't a hope of defeating such a skilful team. The same scene was repeated the length and the breadth of the country. The Nazis could break our bones, but not our spirit or resolve. This picture shows a literally close-knit team.

Bottom: Seen in late November 1941, the brave men and women who defended our freedom take a welcome break from the stark realism of war. They have come in their hundreds to the Sunday Canteen run by the WVS. As well as getting a bite to eat and a cuppa to wash it down, this was a time to meet up with old friends. Perhaps there were some new ones to be made, as well. After all, these were red-blooded British men and women. Such were the times in which they lived that the phrase, 'life is too short', had an unhappily true ring to it. There were papers and magazines to read and a chance to catch up on the news and forces' gossip. Talk centred on the events reported from Gibraltar. The aircraft carrier, HMS Ark Royal, had been lost. Torpedoed by a German submarine, it had been sunk as it made its final run towards the shelter of our foothold on Europe. Worse news was to be on everyone's lips the following week. The Japanese would launch a deadly attack on the American fleet at Pearl Harbour on 7 December. The silver lining to this cloud was that it brought America into the fray. Elsewhere, the Germans were slowing down in their attempt to crush the Russians. Vera Lynn's popular song of the year that there would be, 'Bluebirds over the white cliffs of Dover, just you wait and see' might be coming true, after all.

Right: Jam tarts, scones and sausage rolls - what a choice. So much of it, as well. The Women's Voluntary Service was doing everyone proud at its Sunday Canteen. Pictured at the end of November 1941, these Bedford ladies were doing more than provide refreshments for members of the armed forces. A cup of tea, a piece of cake and a cheery smile was only one small aspect of the work that they did. This was the army that Hitler forgot, to his cost. It was the army of the soul of Britain. Founded in 1938, the WVS was, like Air Raid Precautions, part of the nation's civil defence. Members helped train civilians in the use of gas masks and held first aid classes. At first, thousands flocked to join. Given little to do, many drifted away, but the declaration of war saw the numbers grow again. The Women's Voluntary Service gave support when there were food supply problems, something that was to become more important as the war continued. After a fire or a bombing, the canteen would arrive with a warm meal and hot drink to give refreshment to the emergency services and feed those who had been driven from their homes. These women ran trolley shops in hospitals and cared for the relatives of men who were on the danger list. Their later work in wartime would see a number of them appear on the same danger list. They were no shrinking violets. They were where the action was.

Shopping spree

Looking across High Street, with the market square on the left, the statue of John Howard had been surveying the scene for 55 years since being erected here in 1894 to mark the centenary of the death of the famous reformer in 1890. It honours the work of the nonconformist, born in 1726, who was appalled at the conditions he found in gaols and prison ships. His name is the inspiration behind the Howard League for Penal Reform which continues his good work. Born in nearby Old Harrowden, John Bunyan, the 17th century Puritan and writer, spent time in the 1660s in the County Gaol in High Street. He would have appreciated an earlier birth for Howard! Sir Alfred Gilbert

The statue of John Howard was erected in 1890 to mark the death of the famous reformer

designed the Howard statue. He is best known for his Eros, the centrepiece of London's Piccadilly. Depicted in riding clothes, Howard stands above steps that were once part of the Turnley memorial drinking fountain which was demolished in 1880. John Howard owned Howard House in Mill Street. He helped found a Congregational chapel there in 1772. After a spell as High Sheriff of the county, he travelled all over Britain and Europe. He collected information about prison conditions and vowed to improve them. In 1777 he published the influential 'State of the Prisons in England and Wales'. It was while travelling in the Crimea, visiting military hospitals, that he caught and died from the camp fever which was raging there.

The Americans have taken Iwo Jima and Okinawa. The German Third Reich has only a few weeks to run, but it is market day and some things are more important. By the end of the 20th century, the market would be held twice a week on its riverside site, near the junction of River Street and Horne Lane. In 1945 it hummed and throbbed on St Paul's Square. Money may have been tight and the variety of goods limited in range, but the cries of the stallholders who were encouraging you to buy their wares echoed as enthusiastically as ever. It was also a good place to meet old friends. You were bound to bump into someone you knew who could bring you up to date on the latest titbit of juicy gossip. 'Oooh, she hasn't, has she? Well, I never, and her a Congregationalist, too!' The fine perpendicular Gothic architecture of St Paul's Church dominates the square. It was built in the 14th and 15th centuries. John

Wesley preached from its stone pulpit in 1758. Outside, on the square, is the statue of reformer, John Howard. A statue to another famous son of Bedford, John Bunyan, can be found close to the Saxon tower and Norman door of St Peter's Church. Many a prayer would have been said there in nearly six years of war as mothers and wives quietly knelt and wished for their loved ones to make a safe return. In just a few short weeks, the first of those prayers would be answered.

A glance at the 1950s

WHAT'S ON?
Television hit Britain in a big way during the 1950s. Older readers will surely remember 'Double Your Money', 'Dixon of Dock Green' and 'Dragnet' (whose characters' names were changed 'to protect the innocent'). Commercial television was introduced on 22nd September 1955, and Gibbs SR toothpaste were drawn out of the hat to become the first advert to be shown. Many believed adverts to be vulgar, however, and audiences were far less than had been hoped for.

GETTING AROUND
The year 1959 saw the development of the world's first practical air-cushion vehicle - better known to us as the hovercraft. The earliest model was only able to travel at slow speeds over very calm water and was unable to carry more than three passengers. The faster and smoother alternative to the sea ferry quickly caught on, and by the 1970s a 170-ton car-carrying hover-craft service had been introduced across the English Channel.

SPORTING CHANCE
The four-minute mile had remained the record since 1945, and had become regarded as virtually unbreakable. On 6th May 1954, however, Oxford University student Roger Bannister literally ran away with the record, accomplishing the seemingly impossible in three minutes 59.4 seconds. Bannister collapsed at the end of his last amazing lap, even temporarily losing his vision. By the end of the day, however, he had recovered sufficiently to celebrate his achievement in a London night club!

Above: The railings of St Paul's Churchyard form the left hand edge of the market. The prominent building on the far side of the market square is now a betting shop. Those establishments did not exist in 1945. Bookies' runners used to take betting slips and cash from punters in pubs, street corners and crowded market places, out of sight of the eagle-eyed bobby. Winnings would be passed back in similar fashion. It would not be until the 60s that the betting shop was legalised. The market shoppers had more on their minds than wasting the housekeeping on silly bets. There was the price of vegetables to be argued over and bargains searched out on the fiercely competitive stalls. There was always a chance that an extra root or two could be squeezed out of the seller to make that soup stock go a little further. People came to the market from all over the borough. The town of Bedford and the urban area of Kempston were the obvious centres to which people were attracted. Numerous little settlements, too small to support their own markets, emptied on market day as the villagers came into town. The borough boasts 43 parishes, each comprising one or more villages of various sizes. With petrol rationing in force, the horse and cart, bicycle and good old-fashioned Shanks's pony became regular forms of transport.

Above right: The new Bus Station replaced the one which had operated from The Broadway, a few hundred yards away. In keeping with modern times, the word 'omnibus' was shrunk to 'bus' to make the traveller think that the company was up to date and forward looking in its thinking. The straight lines and sharp edges of the building are typical of the architecture of the period. Planners wanted a clean look, without fancy carvings, turrets or niches. It was also cheaper to erect. That there was no sense of identity did not

worry them. The same design would do for a set of offices or a new school. This was an age of houses like Pete Seeger's 'Little boxes' made of ticky-tacky, that all look just the same. Still, it looked clean and bright in September 1961. From the back of British Home Stores, we are looking across Church Square, towards Allhallows. This was part of a new shopping development. Eventually, the centre of Bedford would be pedestrianised as Silver Street connected High Street with the Harpur Centre and the Howard Centre. Church Square is known to local residents as 'Pigeon Square'. The attractions of the birds that frequent the square are more than offset by the mess they leave on the buildings, street and your overcoat. The official name of the square comes from the Church family of bakers in St Loyes St. It was originally applied to a group of cottages which once stood here.

At work

Below: Readers in the new millennium can look at this scene and say, quite rightly, that this is an example of technology in an earlier millennium. It shows an age of hand-cranked field telephones, jack plugs, wires and jumbled cables everywhere. There is not a microchip or transistor in sight. 'Digital' would have meant using your finger to plug in the connection, to this member of the Women's Auxiliary Police Force. Before we scoff at the antiquated equipment, let us remember that a machine is only as useful as the operator allows it to be. The most powerful computer, in the hands of a dunce, is of no use at all. This woman was no fool. Skilfully using her bank of phones and little switchboard, she could relay information back and forth to police cars and nerve centres across the county. She was the backroom brains behind the communications that directed messages to the bobbies. Without her, they were lost. She was the first port of call in an emergency. It was the use of her initiative that

sparked speedy and appropriate response. A computer is just a tool; it is the human who has the intelligence. In this war, women were actively recruited for work. One campaign quoted Seaman Gunner John Reid MN saying, 'We can do our jobs, if you do yours.' Women needed little encouragement. Before the hostilities began, they had been ready. Lady Stella Reading had founded the WVS in 1938 and the Women's Auxiliary Air Force came into being in July 1939.

Bottom: Mission impossible? Not for this young woman of the Women's Auxiliary Police Force in July 1942. She may be on her way with sealed instructions for a superior officer or about to deliver a summons to some wayward individual. Whatever it was, it would be done efficiently and quickly. The roles of women in both World Wars advanced the cause of universal suffrage more than any demonstration by Mrs Pankhurst. In World War I, men had come to accept the sight of the female ambulance driver and the production line worker. During the 1939-45 conflict, their contribution to winning the war would increase dramatically. Volunteers flocked to join the Air Force, Police, Civil Defence and Land Army. This was in addition to all those who took over factory and office jobs, relinquished by men who had moved up to the front lines. No longer would there ever be a traditional 'man's job'. Let us face it. Men had made such a mess of the world in the first half of the 20th century that it was time for a change in attitude. Women had been 'her indoors' for too long. Even so, it was still a far cry from being in the thick of the fighting. Men in the armed forces would resist the attempts of any coming close to seeing action, other than nurses, that is. It was all right to risk them. They were useful in patching up the men.

From the Crimea to Chalks and Crayons

As an Aide-de-Campe in the Crimea Joseph Binney not only witnessed the spectacular Charge of the Light Brigade but survived the miseries of campaigning in a freezing winter and two cholera ridden summers. In 1860 he moved to the vast, still rural state of New York where, in the last year of the bitter Civil War, he established the Peekskill Chemical Works. The firm first produced pharmaceutical charcoal for medical use and three years later, in New York City, started the distribution of charcoal, lamp black (for burnishing cast iron cooking ranges), paints and colours imported from Europe.

His son Edwin, born 1866, and nephew C H Smith both joined him in the early 1880s, when they received a rigorous training in salesmanship prior to Joseph's retirement in 1885, after which the two cousins took control of the growing company which was renamed Binney & Smith. They added shoe polish, black pigments, printing inks and crayons to the existing lines using carbon black, a totally new by product made from the natural gas taken from the early oilfields in the industrialised state of Pennsylvania.

While C H Smith travelled the world selling carbon black and its products to Chinese lacquer

work producers and European paint makers alike Edwin Binney ran the company and developed the new lines which are today the mainstay of this international company. One of these was the wax crayon, which has since coloured the world for nearly a hundred years, sold under the Crayola trademark invented by Edwin's French wife Alice, a former teacher, derived from the words 'craie' (chalk) and 'ola' (oily). The year 1903 saw the first packet of Crayola crayons emerge, this was a box of eight and sold in America only for the price of a nickel.

During the Great War Britain found itself short of many items formerly imported from the innovative German chemical industry. In 1916 Binney & Smith, in liaison with another American firm of crayon manufacturers, established the Cosmic Crayon Company.

The declaration of peace was followed, in 1919, by a company move to Bedford in search of larger premises. Binney & Smith took over what they considered a most unlikely building for an industrial enterprise which was, however, surrounded by eighteen acres of grounds. Obviously the firm had an eye to future expansion! This was the former premises of the grandly named Bedford Middle Class Public School, originally run by a clergyman for the sons of priests and others of that ilk. His brother, South African diamond millionaire Sir George Farrar, had generously funded the enterprise.

During the Great War the vastly expanded Royal Flying Corps had commandeered the school's splendid building and sports grounds for use as an OCTU (Officer Cadet Training Unit) which, following the post war run down of the newly formed RAF, was returned to its owner.

***Above centre:** An early display of Crayola Crayons.*
***Top:** JW Binney (1836 - 1898), founder of the world famous company.*

Awakening to the wonderful world of color

Inspire the secret dreams and bold accomplishments
that only children know. Give them the means to
explore and relight your own glad memories. Act soon
...before the dreams of youth escape, beyond recapture.

...*remember?*

As he was too ill to continue the business the Rev Farrar sold it to the Cosmic Crayon Company in 1919 for use as their European factory.

Originally mixed by hand in small batches with a colour range limited to eight pigments, Crayola crayons were each covered in a matching paper wrapper. Modern users of Crayola wax crayons can select from seventy-two different colours including eight that the company attempted to

Above: *An early example of magazine advertising, this one aimed at the American market.*

retire in 1991 which were, however, saved by public protest! School teachers prefer the high standard Crayola products to the cheaper substitutes introduced by cost conscious administrators. Binney & Smith Anti-Dust dust-free black board chalks, both white and coloured, last much longer and do not break so readily as the dusty inferior makes which swiftly crumble in use by traditional 'chalk and talk' teachers. Proof indeed that the Crayola quality achieved by using first class raw materials and sound manufacturing processes produces a product which pays for any slight cost differential many times over. Local Education Authority buyers should heed those at the 'chalk face' and insist on Crayola Anti-Dust. Bedford in the 1950s was one of the few towns in

> *School teachers prefer the high standards of Crayola to the cheaper imitations introduced recently*

England to have both an Italian Consulate, and an Italian cinema, to cater for the large population of Italians living and working in the vicinity. Originally recruited from a few villages in Italy for jobs in Bedford based brickworks many of these cheerful, hard working, temporary contract workers settled down. They, and their descendants, soon expanded their employment ambitions as some ran restaurants for Bedfordians tentatively experimenting with foreign food and others learned new skills with firms such as Binney & Smith.

During the expansive years of the 1950s the restrictions set on production by the layout of a late Victorian boarding school building were

Top: *The Cosmic Crayon Company's headquarters in Bedford until 1964.*

It has long been the practice at Binney & Smith to foster company loyalty by offering long service awards for those who worked there for three years upwards. During the 1998 Award Presentation Ceremony the thirty Bedford based employees honoured for their commitment, loyalty and long service had amassed a combined total of 394 years employment with the company.

Even in the best of companies things can go wrong due to revolutions, Acts of God and other unexpected factors. Binney & Smith remember well the fire of 10th August 1975, which destroyed three quarters of the proud new factory which had superseded the late Victorian school in 1964. As paraffin wax and oils are inflammable the fire was disastrous. The local fire brigades took two days of hectic water pumping to douse the burning raw materials. There was no loss of life during this event which had deposited a six inch residue of multi-coloured wax where rivers of water had carried it

increasingly apparent. Business efficiency and economic product methods called for a modern purpose built facility which duly arrived in 1964. This modern looking glass fronted, two storey factory was constructed on the former school playing field with the old school building being demolished in late 1964 after it was sold to another local company, Robinson Rentals.

Above left: The Bedford factory production line in the mid 1980s. Below: A picture taken at Earls Court Toy Fair in January 1983 with from left to right - John Anderson (former employee), Mike Smith (former MD now Chairman Arts & Education Board) Tom Baker (former Dr Who), Dave Barker (present MD) and Jerry McFadden (Binney & Smith employee in the Far East).

during its molten state. Three weeks hard work were needed to remove this before work could start in what remained of the premises.

The next tasks were to make safe the roof covering the undamaged sections and to restore heating and electric power to the office block from which essential contact with suppliers, distributors and customers was maintained. Although the boiler house was one hundred yards from the office this was achieved using a temporary steam pipe connection. By October the Chalk Department was back in production, protected from the autumnal weather by tarpaulins spread over the roof, showing that the English are at their dogged best in times of adversity. 'Business as Usual' was the motto as temporary homes were found for other departments. The Wax

Department and Shipping Area were billeted three quarters of a mile away at Austin Canons on the Kempston Road, now the site of the North Beds and Herts Ambulance Station.

New packaging and labelling machines were installed so that unlabelled crayons, imported from the Crayola works in the USA, could be labelled with English labels. For some nine months this job was undertaken by the three shifts working at Austin Canons while the Ampthill Road buildings were rebuilt in time for a return in September 1976. Prior to the fire the English company concentrated on supplying chalks and crayons to schools and colleges throughout the British Isles and the developing countries of the Commonwealth. The former sales were in decline partly due to changes in teaching methods and partly due to

Above centre: *Crayola - 1999 style!*
Top: *The Bedford staff in a recent photograph.*

1950s and 1960s, curious as the Crayola brand was not launched in the UK until 1973! Previously Binney & Smith had used a variety of brands including Cosmic and Finart.

The company's continued success and impressive growth has been based on some fundamental and simple basic philosophies, which are at the very core of their organisation. By empowering their people to make a real difference in their everyday job decision making, it creates a partnership between employer and employee which not only stands the test of time but also motivates high performance and pride. Tremendous employee loyalty and dedication has been at the heart of Binney & Smith for as long as anyone can remember.

Investing and focusing on the Crayola brand for more than a generation has resulted in tremendous consumer loyalty from mothers particularly, who are the key purchasers of Crayola products for their children. Mothers know and trust the Crayola brand to deliver excellent quality, safe, well designed, age appropriate, innovative products at fair prices.

Building on the heritage of crayons, the 1980s saw the launch of coloured pencils and special 'washable' inks for childrens' colouring pens along with a whole range of dazzling art cases and storage systems.

The future for Binney & Smith looks very bright as the company continues to reach out to consumers in ever more imaginative and innovative ways. But, at the heart of the company, both in the past, now and in the future, lies a deep and unshakeable desire to play a profound role in the life of children aged two to twelve as they grow from scribbling with their first crayons or paintbrush to mastering the art of colouring 'between the lines' and finally truly expressing themselves with colour and creativity.

Above right: *The Crayola stand at a recent exhibition.*

reduced public funding while the latter suffered from the uncertainties of intermittent development.

Crayola, in common with other manufacturers, cannot stand still but has to continue making and selling old and new products. Of the four hundred and eighty four products developed by Binney & Smith since 1864 some 47 percent are still sold! Clients such as farmers mark sheep and cattle with Binney & Smith crayons, fishermen camouflage their nets by colouring them with similar crayons and, more expectedly, artists in all commercial fields have used Crayola crayons since 1903. Even so there was scope for improvement to fill the gap left by declining school sales. In 1981, after years of steady but relatively unspectacular growth the company began a bold expansion strategy to truly capitalise on the power of the Crayola brandname. A much more aggressive sales and marketing strategy was implemented to target mainstream retailers of childrens' stationery and toy products. Crayola Creative Activities were born, to capture this marketplace with gift sets of all shapes and sizes, all attractively priced in familiar yellow and green Crayola packaging. An interesting and recurring fact throughout Crayola product history is that mothers continually claim to have used Crayola crayons themselves as children throughout the

Funerals for the future

Every society has its own, often unique, traditions for dealing with death while the more enlightened provide much needed support for those left behind. The customs in some societies often seem strange to those accustomed to the peaceful dignity of an English funeral service. As death comes to every one but once in a lifetime the form of remembrance and interment can be of great comfort to the relatives and friends.

It is at such times that the assistance offered by Arnold's Funeral Service can relieve the strain imposed on grieving families. There is an enormous volume of legal and financial work which relatives have to undertake on the death of a loved one. Dealing with the Registrar to record the death and obtain Death Certificates is one thing, as are the matters of Wills and investments, but arranging a funeral is an affair that many prefer to leave in the

hands of professionals. Arnolds are experienced in organising both burials and cremations in order to relieve grieving families of the additional distress of arranging these themselves.

Bedford, in common with many similar towns, is fortunate in having a public cemetery to supplement the town's collection of churchyards. The latter provided a final resting place for many generations of Bedfordians whose memorial stones, plaques and stained glass windows provide family and local historians alike with details of past lives and achievements. Fortunately the urban population

explosion of Victorian times was matched by the rapid development both of funeral services and of town cemeteries.

The earliest part of Neville Funeral Service in Ampthill was founded in 1875 by Thomas and Edward Neville who established themselves in Castle Street, Luton. It was the practice for several generations to combine undertaking with another allied enterprise. In the case of Neville Funeral Service their alternative enterprise was Building, in those days a trade rather more at the mercy of the seasons than it is today. As more deaths in the last quarter century of Queen Victoria's reign tended to occur during the colder winter months this part of the business fitted in well with fine weather building activities.

Neville Funeral Service stayed almost a century in Luton until 1967 during which time they made the magnificent coffins of durable English hardwoods like Elm and Oak. As Elm trees were decimated by the ravages of Dutch Elm Disease many of the solid wood coffins nowadays are made of Oak, for those who prefer traditional materials. As many people now share a concern for the environment the more economic veneered chipboard, and even cardboard coffins provide a sensible alternative. These environmentally friendly coffins may, of course, be adorned with the same interior and memorial plates as the solid wood versions.

Throughout the Middle Ages the law decreed that the dead were wrapped in a shroud of good wool cloth before burial. This measure was designed to foster the national weaving trade at a time when much of the wool clip was exported to weavers in Italy and the Low Countries. Some people today consider that coffins of woven wicker are just the thing for rapid recycling of coffin and contents, whether these be cremated or buried.

Neville Funeral Service next moved to Marsh Road,

Left: The Roff Avenue premises pictured in the early 1950s.

Leagrave, on the edge of Luton, still their head office, and have since expanded to additional premises in Ampthill, a pretty Georgian town which has grown considerably. They bought an attractive, redundant church with land for car parking and room for building additional facilities. Here they can offer clients a service worthy of the Millennium of the Nativity of our Lord.

Neville Funeral Service operates throughout Bedfordshire but it also provides a service between Britain and Ireland for the many families of Irish extraction who came to England either to settle down or to undertake temporary work. More recent migrants to Britain are those who have left India and Pakistan in search of work in a climate and

Both pictures: *Recent funerals combining a mix of modern vehicles and a horse drawn hearse.*

culture so different to that left behind. It is not surprising that these peoples, all with strong religious traditions and close knit family ties, should choose to return home after death. Their relatives regard it as a matter of honour that the deceased should be mourned, and their body buried, in accor-

dance with their unique customs. Many repatriations are made at the express wish of persons desiring to be buried in a place of which they have fond memories or are of great religious significance to their beliefs.

In Bedford itself Leonard CJ Arnold, an Apprentice Carpenter and Joiner, followed the old custom of training as an undertaker in addition to these crafts.

This extensive course added two years to the length of his training which proved to be the foundation of the Arnold family business. In 1955 he was in a position to set up, with his family, as his own boss as a Carpenter/Joiner at 48 Park Road East, which has since been renamed Roff Avenue. As is so often the case in family business ventures Mrs B Arnold provided the vital secretarial expertise assisted by their daughter Miss B Arnold. Their son Mr K Arnold also worked in the funeral business.

Customers are thankful for the generations of family expertise for a professional service

The company stayed in Park Road East for thirty-eight years and, six years later, were still at the same premises in the renamed Roff Avenue. As horse-drawn vehicles were common in the 1950s it is no surprise that Arnolds employed horse-drawn hearses. In time these magnificent and stately creatures were replaced by handsome Daimlers and other purpose built vehicles. More recently the horse has returned to popularity as hearses drawn by traditional teams of handsome black horses have added a touch of nostalgia to funeral processions.

Arnolds employ well trained, qualified staff capable of providing both traditional and modern styles of service. The respect shown both to the deceased and the bereaved is vital to the spirit of those left behind as a well run funeral greatly eases the pain of the mourners. Fortunately Arnold's

Above: The old church at Ampthill when Arnold's first acquired it.

customers have every reason to be thankful that they can rely on several generations of family expertise for a professional operation.

Such expertise extends to the company's own floristry department where the floral tributes are made using flowers selected by mourners. These can reflect either personal favourites or flowers with historic and religious meanings to add significance to the event. Where desired Arnolds will provide the catering to suit the occasion.

Above: *A funeral by Neville Funeral Services in Ampthill.*

After many years of independent trading Neville Funeral Service acquired LCJ Arnolds Funeral Directors so that they could operate on a county wide scale from their premises in Ampthill, Bedford and Luton. Although the Arnold joinery business was dropped in favour of a total dedication to funeral directing, everyone worked together to provide the best service for the bereaved available in Bedfordshire. Because Bedford is home to many of the Italians who came to work in the local brick-works, and who have since made niches for themselves in other fields, there is a demand for a repatriation service to take the deceased home to Italy. There they can be interred, according to their

customs, in cemeteries patronised by their families who will maintain the graves or tombs.

Some people prefer a funeral to be conducted without any religious reference or ceremony at all. Nature lovers and conservationists find comfort in the simple and natural style of a Woodland burial. Whatever the desires of the customers Arnolds are able to provide a traditional or modern service with both respect and economy.

Peter Aspinall is managing director and his sensitive book 'To Shed A Light', written from the viewpoint of the deceased concerned by the trauma experienced by their closest family, is full of sound advice. Representatives of the company who visit people in their own homes to discuss the organisation of a funeral often

find that they are dealing with a person making arrangements for themselves in order to save their family extra heartache. If this foresight appeals to you be assured that the matter will be conducted in the greatest confidence in order to protect loved ones from any foreboding which might arise from a desire to save them pain.

Top left: *Neville Funeral Service premises in Ampthill.* ***Below:*** *Arnolds Funeral Service premises as they look today.*

Bedford - the backbone of the motor industry

Lynton Works, on Ampthill Road, Bedford, has played an important role in the industrial development of Bedford throughout virtually the whole of the 20th century. With a succession of names above the door, and a variety of products leaving the factory, it has, with barely an interruption, provided employment for the townsfolk ever since 1907; today, operating as part of a major international group of companies employing some 170,000 worldwide, of whom some 400 are employed at Bedford, Lynton Works is in a stronger position than ever to rise to meet the new challenges which the next century will bring.

The first person to engage in manufacturing at Lynton Works was W H A Robertson, who in 1907 constructed and equipped a 1,000 square foot workshop where he employed a workforce of five to make wire drawing and nail forming machinery. The company prospered and grew, maintaining its position in the industry as a family-owned business throughout the two wars, and then, in 1953, joined the Tube Investments Group. As Principal Capital Goods manufacturer of the TI Engineering Division, Lynton Works enjoyed continued expansion and product

Below: *Graf Borer - Vauxhall Motors.*
Bottom: *Machine die castings.*

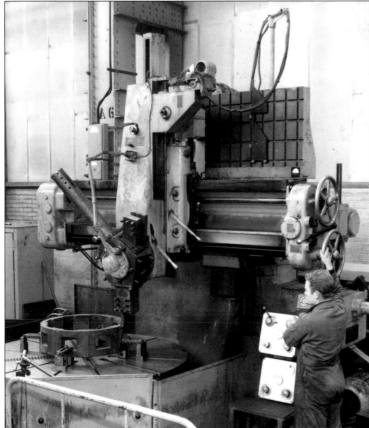

manufactured under the Robertson name for customers world-wide. By 1966 the number of employees had risen to 1,250 and the factory floor area had grown to its current size of 200,000 square feet, permitting the manufacture of very large plant installations; that same year saw the production of the largest installation yet produced at Lynton Works, a Hallden Robertson flying shear weighing over 250 tons and occupying 1,000 square feet of floor area. This powerful machine, using the latest technology of the day, was capable of cutting mild steel three-eighths of an inch thick in widths of up to 72 inches at speeds of up to 350 feet a minute, cost around £300,000 and was made for the Australian Iron & Steel Company's plant at Port Kembla, New South Wales.

Later in the decade the company came under the umbrella of the Davy United Engineering Groups, and operations at Lynton Works were subsequently brought to a halt. Fortunately, however, the plant did not remain closed for long; in May 1969 it re-opened as Division 454, part of the Tool & Die Division of Vauxhall Motors, Luton. Of the 11 acre site, the Tool & Die manufacturing facility occupied a floor space of 190,000 square feet. Once again a wide range of

development, with a wide range of engineering equipment - steel rolling mills, shearline equipment, metal forming equipment, and, rather ironically, presses for the automotive industry - being

This page: *Vauxhall Motors small mill shop general machining.*

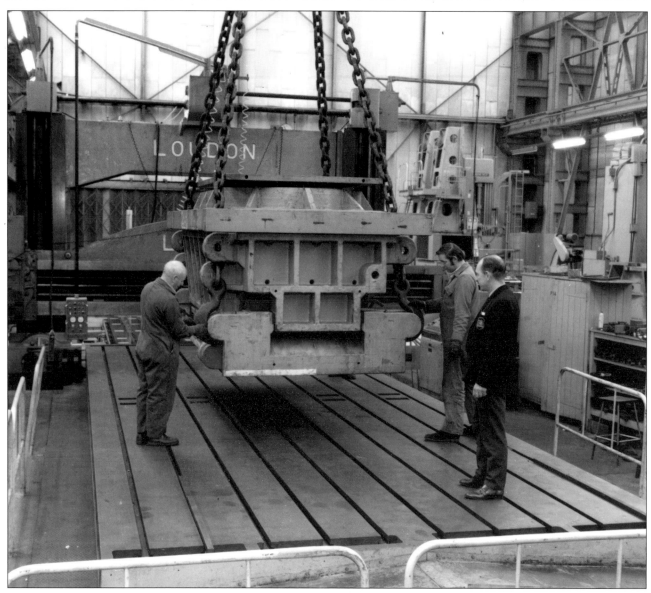

engineering work was carried out, this time for the automotive industry: press tool construction, tool tryout, jigs, fixtures and multiweld equipment; the late 1960s and 70s were an era when car ownership was soaring, and the automotive industry was expanding rapidly. In addition to this, some large machining work was undertaken for outside customers - using equipment which had been installed during the Robertson era.

Lynton Works remained Vauxhall Motors' Division 454 until 1970 and then the plant was retained by General Motors but was renamed the Bedford Tool & Die Plant. Under this name it continued to produce a significant proportion of the whole range of body stamping dies for Vauxhall and Bedford vehicles, working on projects including the Cavalier, the Astra and the Astra van, the CF van, the Chevanne, and military trucks. While its customer base consisted mainly of General Motors plants engaged in the manufacture of both cars and trucks in Europe, a certain amount of work was also carried out for both domestic and overseas clients outside the Group. This manufacture was to remain the basis of the Bedford Tool & Die Plant's activities until March 1985. At the peak of its activities some 600 skilled

Above and top: *Robertsons Louden planer machining fabrications.*

men and a further 80 or so support team personnel were employed there. During most of this period the plant manager was Bob Simpkins, who will not only be remembered by former employees but will be well known to many other readers besides as he is still resident in Bedford.

March 1985 signified the end of another era at Lynton Works. The plant ceased operating as General Motors' tooling division, and from 1st April that year Pre-Star, part of the Camford Engineering Group, took over the site, retaining the existing personnel.

Pre-Star had been started in Luton in 1964, specialising in the manufacture of basic components for the motor industry, from U-bolts and castings to side members and body panels. The Company was floated on the stock exchange in 1972 and became Camford Engineering plc. It grew rapidly, both through expansion and through acquisition; within 10 years it had become one of Britain's largest manufacturers of automotive components, employing some 2,000 people at nine major plants in the UK. In addition to the original Pre-Star (Luton) plant, the Group at this stage included J Simpson & Son of Luton, Geo W King of Stevenage, the subsidiary company U Bolts (Pre-Star) Ltd which was set up at Luton specifically to manufacture U-bolts, a foundry at Hemel

Hempstead, a manufacturing plant at Bourn (Cambridge), and extensive bulk storage and distribution facilities at Luton, Southampton and Bedford. The Group's main focus was on supplying the assembly lines of car and truck manufacturers at home and abroad and its activities were concentrated on high-volume production of an unusually wide range of automotive components and assemblies, although it also had clients outside the automotive industry such as Shell, BP, the Post Office, Black & Decker and British Railways.

On taking over the Lynton Works on 1st April 1985, the Camford Engineering Group set up a new independent company called Lynton Tool & Die under the Camford Group umbrella, and tool manufacture continued under this name. The remainder of the site operated as Pre-Star (Luton), initially manufacturing a comprehensive range of fabricated and pressed components and component assemblies for use in cars produced for the UK and European markets; the range included latch assemblies, seat frames, body panels and pillars, brake systems, petrol tanks and axle cases. In the years which followed, a number of external factors combined to create an economic climate which posed many challenges for the automotive industry, and the Camford Group became the subject of financial interest from a succession of parties. Despite these uncertainties, production at Lynton

Works continued under the Pre-Star name, with production now concentrated on chassis and suspension components.

In August 1989 the company was awarded the prestigious R8 contract by Rover for the manufacture of rear and front cross-members, and their excellent performance in carrying out this project made them 'natural choice' when plans were made for the model's successor, the new Rover 200. Pre-Star began working on the R3 project for the successful Rover 200 in October 1995, and this commitment will continue into the year 2001, with Pre-Star contracted to supply annual volumes of 165,000 rear and 85,000 front cross-members over a period of six years.

Camford Engineering lost a hostile take-over by Markheath Securities in 1991 who, after retaining three prime freehold sites, subsequently sold the remaining manufacturing plants, which included Bedford, to Hoesch. Hoesch was a German steel-making and automotive component supply company based in Dortmund, Germany. Following the merger of Hoesch with Krupp (who had a similar supply base to Hoesch) the Camford Group was taken under

the wing of Krupp Hoesch Automotive. Meanwhile Pre-Star had been re-structured, with the Bourn site being merged with Lynton Works in 1991 and production switched exclusively to chassis and suspension parts on state-of-the-art press lines with

Above: Machining body shape dies.
Top: A die sinker at Vauxhall.

transfer systems and robot welders. The following year Pre-Star, now employing a total workforce of 750 at its two sites, began producing the suspension frame for the Sierra replacement at Lynton Works. Further recognition of the company's high standards of excellence followed when Pre-Star was nominated by Ford as the sole European source of the front suspension frame for the BE91 Fiesta replacement, with Lynton Works responsible for supplying Ford's Dagenham plant. In addition Pre-Star was appointed to manufacture the suspension beam for the new Honda Synchro. Part of Pre-Star's competitive advantage lay in its advanced

Camford Limited, with the Lynton site the Bedford division.

Further achievements since have included ISO 9000 quality awards and Full Service Supplier status from Ford.

Moves towards a merger between Krupp and Thyssen began early in 1998 and were finalised on March 17th 1999, and at the time of writing Lynton Works is looking forward to one more change of name before the end of this millennium. As TKA or ThyssenKrupp Automotive Chassis Products UK, part of a major group which

technology; it was the sole licensee of the T1 Variform process in the UK, using the hydroforming process developed by Krupp Camford which results in lighter weight, lower cost components, offering significant benefits to customers. So, with official recognition by Ford, close links with Rover and growing connections with other manufacturers, Pre-Star's position at the forefront of the industry was now assured for the future. In 1996 the Pre-Star name was dropped and the Company renamed Krupp

operates in the global market place where it ranks amongst the world's industrial elite, the factory which began as a little workshop in 1907 with a workforce of five, and whose survival and dynamic growth has contributed so much to Bedford's prosperity and industrial development, will continue its tradition of engineering excellence into the next era.

Above: *The Bedford plant.*
Below: *The Krupp Camford Rover 200 launch team.*

Success to the Brave

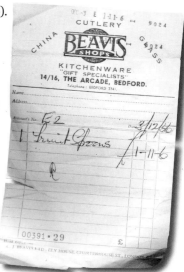

CJ Beavis Ltd has a company history to rivet any family historian to their chair. A stirring tale of family endeavour ranging from high success to courageous survival against all odds when others, unable to beat the giants of business, fell by the wayside . Bedfordians will know well Beavis' Bedford shops for their imaginative, tasteful and ever changing stock of gifts, china, crystal and cards. Shops to enhance any shopping centre and to attract customers through the doors time and time again.

CJ Beavis Ltd dates back to 1934 but before that the same family built up and owned the Domestic Bazaar Company or DBC, as it was familiarly known throughout the land. The first of the DBC empire of shops was opened in Portsmouth by Albert Octavius Beavis and his three brothers in 1895 and quickly earned the name 'Mr Tanner' as everything was sold

for a 'tanner', ie 6d (2.5p). The stock in trade of those early years was kitchen ware and household utensils aimed at the lower end of the market, hence the swings and round-abouts pricing.

So effective was their marketing in the last years of the Queen Empress' long reign and the all too short Edwardian Summer which followed that the family had 190 shops by the 1920s. The Bedford branch of three shop units was opened in 1905 when the Arcade was first built. Their empire covered major towns from Inverness to Penzance, which were supplied, in part, from their own tin

Above left: Cecil James Beavis, founder of the company. Above right: An early receipt. Below: The shop in the early 1950s when managed by Donald James Beavis.

kettle factory in Birmingham. They also had a number of travelling caravans, supplied by rail from the Midlands, taking their goods to the smaller market towns along the East Coast to sell to country people on market days. No wonder shopping in the past was such a pleasure when wonderful entrepreneurs such as the Beavis brothers brought useful items within walking distance of home.

All went swimmingly, as the Beavis DBC shops and vans brought well deserved wealth to the family, until 1930 when a forceful, gung ho Yankee competitor invaded Britain. The enormously rich Woolworth family recognised the true worth of the DBC and offered to buy the family out on very generous terms which included shares in Woolworth's. The wealthy self-made Beavis brothers rejected the partnership and immediately found themselves in a fierce trading battle. Whereever there was a DBC shop Woolworths opened up one of their own on the other side of the road and under-priced everything by a penny. When selling cut price goods at the lower end of the market only those with deep pockets can

win that sort of fight and after two years the Beavis brothers had to fling in the towel.

Out of the wreckage, which followed the unpleasant hiatus of 'going into receivership' and the retirement of the founder, Albert Octavius Beavis and his three brothers. Cecil James Beavis, A O's eldest son, a wartime RFC officer, was able to rescue only five former DBC shops. In 1934 he bravely leased from the Official Receiver the shops in Bedford, Wolverhampton, Stoke Newington, London, Crouch End, Essex and Newport on the Isle of Wight. These were strategically placed to make a come-back against almighty odds but CJ was in the position of David if he'd been KO'd by Goliath. What was his next move to be? To make matters worse Britain was in the grip of The Depression when professional men were glad to take menial jobs and others existed on the dole for a decade. A tough time indeed to attempt a comeback!

It was achieved by CJ persuading his family and the shop managers to back him to the tune of £4,600, equivalent to about nine years' salary for a bank manager in the days when many families lived comfortably on £200 a year. Miss Florence Adelaide Edwards, the manageress of Bedford, courageously invested £100 which covered the first six month's rent! Nowadays that costs some £15,000. The reborn firm paid its manageresses four times the going rate for the shop assistants while CJ received four times the manageress' salary but not for every one of the five shops. By comparison the present owner receives only thrice the pay of his shop staff as pay differentials have been considerably eroded by time and economics.

Above left: *An early Beavis van.*
Top: *Left to right: CJ Beavis, IC Beavis (youngest son), AO Beavis (father).*

As Woolworths were here to stay as the 'thru'penny and six-penny' store the new firm of Beavis upgraded its lines of china and glass, cutlery and hardware to attract a different class of customer. The new business prospered so that within a year a sixth shop was opened in the hilly market town of Guildford. Donald James Beavis (CJ's eldest son) entered Bedford School in 1935 and during his years there he met his future wife, then a pupil at Bedford High School for girls. In 1940 the Head Office was moved from the Blitz battered capital to rooms above Achille Serre, cleaners at 103 High Street (now Walton's Estate Agents). The second world war was an odd time for shops of this type as although people were eager to buy replacement kitchen and tableware, not to mention wedding gifts, supplies of non-essentials were severely restricted as manufacturers concentrated on the war effort.

When production returned to normal people queued, whenever lorries unloaded crates of straw packed china and glass at the entrance to The Arcade, and waited for the chance to replenish their depleted household stocks with whatever was unloaded.

To everyone's surprise in 1946, the first year of peace, DJ found himself conscripted into the Army for four years. When he returned he took over the Bedford shop

Top: *Left to right: DJ Beavis, CJ Beavis, Mrs MA Beavis (DJ's wife), Mrs EM Beavis (CJ's wife), IC Beavis.* **Above right:** *The Industrial and Trades Exhibition of 1950.*

and married his boyhood sweetheart who gave birth to their son Michael in 1952. Also in 1950 CJ's youngest son, Ian Cecil Beavis entered Bedford School and on leaving joined the family business and started up the new branch at Leicester in 1959, and currently owns the Newport shop. Once rationing had at last finished the bright years following the Queen's Coronation in 1953 saw Britain enjoy full employment as businesses, including Beavis, expanded at full steam ahead under the Conservative government headed by Winston Churchill and later PMs. During this decade Beavis formed a wholesale subsidiary in the Isle of Wight which between 1953 and 1982 provided caterers with kitchenware, tableware and glassware.

Beavis opened a series of additional shops in the Isle of Wight in the 50s and 60s followed by one in Halford Street, Leicester (1959), and a greetings card shop at 19 The Arcade in Bedford in 1962. The redoubtable CJ retired in 1966 when the reins passed to his sons, DJ and IC, who shut down loss making branches at Guildford (1966), Wolverhampton and Stoke Newington in 1967 and Crouch End in 1974. These closures were matched by expansion elsewhere as the company adapted to changing circumstances until a total of ten shops, a warehouse and head office was reached with duplicate branches in Leicester (1971), which aimed at the younger customer, and the ever buoyant Isle of Wight.

New ventures included shops selling deep freezers, imported from Sweden, and frozen food with which to fill them. When stainless steel cutlery became popular

Beavis established a warehouse for centralised purchasing and marketed their own brand of cutlery and china for a period.

The early 1980s saw trading bedevilled by the recession which killed off many other businesses both new and old. In 1980 the lease on Halford Street, Leicester, the most profitable shop in the chain, expired. The family made the decision to move to other premises at Market Place South in Leicester which provided 30 percent more space in a busier location. The same year that this decision was made saw an 11 percent reduction in turnover, with a higher rent to pay, followed by a further decrease in 1981 while the other branches were in a similarly parlous position.

Drastic surgery was applied in 1982 to save the business as all outstations were closed except for the two Bedford shops and the three Isle of Wight shops under two separate management units of DJ and IC. DJ's son and heir, Michael went to work in a department store in Surrey for ten years until returning in 1992 to take over from his father, Donald James Beavis, who had concentrated on the giftware trade. Since then the Bedford shops have focussed on popular series of collectables which many people add to as each item is produced. Customer interest is maintained by a strict policy of updating good quality stock with new lines and rigorously culling the 'stickers' at sale prices. Repeat buyers benefit from the firm's new loyalty scheme which represents 23 percent of sales. Remember for choice and value, Better Buy Beavis.

Left and below: *The shop today.*

George Fischer Ltd- From ploughs to pipe fittings at Cauldwell Priory

The ancient grounds of the former Priory of Cauldwell, founded in 1200 AD and adjacent to the River Ouse, became in the 1850s, the largest site in the world for the manufacture of agricultural implements.

James and Fredrick Howard, the sons of John Howard, who for many years had carried on business in the town as an ironmonger purchased some 20 acres on which to construct a factory. Designed by Robert Palgrove, later 'Sir' following his work on the extensions to Buckingham Palace, the factory opened on 3rd February 1859 and was named 'Britannia Works'. The Gate House which still stands was likened by the contemporary press as "The portal of some symbolic castle of indolence on some luxurious place of learning,

anything indeed but a temple of industry". Howards prospered over the years and were pioneers in the introduction of ploughing by steam power and received many awards and gold medals for their products at various international exhibitions, especially at the Great Exhibitions in London and Paris. Much was written of them in engineering journals of the time.

Many eminent persons from all over the world visited their Works including General Garibaldi, the liberator of Italy, who planted a tree in commemoration of his visit. Prince Albert (Queen Victoria's husband) was also due to visit but died before this could be accomplished.

Above: *Britannia Iron Works - 1874.*
Below: *The Foundry c1958.*

Fischer had been searching for a suitable factory in this country to produce their range of malleable iron fittings and so avoid the high import duty imposed during the difficult years of the Great Depression in this country. So Britannia Works rose again, albeit under the new name of Britannia Iron and Steel Works.

The foundry was modernised, new annealing furnaces built, specialised screwing machines tools installed and

Over the years many 1,000's of ploughs and tillage implements were exported all over the world. Following the 1914-18 war and a merger with other manufacturers Howards business slowly declined and closure came on the 15th February 1932 with some 500 workers losing their jobs.

Following the closure of Howards the works were put up for sale and purchased in October 1932 by Edward le Bas, acting on behalf of George Fischer Schaffhausen, Switzerland. George

other ancillary departments added. The first melt under the new George Fischer ownership was made on 26 August 1933, when approximately 250 people were employed, many ex Howards workers. In 1934 the average weekly wage was £27s 6d (£2.37 1/2 p). In the late 1930s production of castings for customers' special requirements was commenced and during the second world war large amounts of tank tracks

Above left: Products leaving the Works in the 1960s.
Top: Selection of malleable iron fittings.

and castings for fighting vehicles were manufactured. After the war, this was developed further into supplying castings in a variety of grades of Malleable Cast Iron for automobiles, agricultural machinery, machine tools, railways and many other industries.

By 1950 the workforce had risen to 750 and peaked at just over 1,000 in the 1960s. Extension to the foundry was made in 1952 to accommodate expanding fittings and castings requirements. Output continued to grow and in 1966 an entirely new foundry was commissioned. This George Fischer Buehrer automatic plant was a six station rotary moulding unit that replaced the old 'Jolt Squeeze' moulding machines in use at the time. The new machines were capable of producing some 300 moulds per hour and some 5,000 tons per year on a single shift. In 1975 the two cupola furnaces used to produce the liquid metal were further modified to comply with 'Clean Air Act' and a tall chimney was added to disperse the cleaned smoke.

In 1971, the Company name was changed to

George Fischer Castings Limited to reflect a more up to date company image.

In 1990, some 12.6 million screwed fittings were manufactured at the Bedford plant amounting to 2,960 tons plus 1300 tons of customer castings and 770 tons of Distribution Products.

In 1992 the change in market conditions made the large Bedford site uneconomical and the

Below: *Drawing molten metal from a cupola furnace.*
Bottom: *The Machine Shop in the 1950s.*

castings still required for the product range are supplied by a UK foundry based in the Birmingham area. The new Company employing 50 people machines the castings to the required shape and together with additional components obtained from other suppliers assembles the fittings to customer requirements. The Company is also very actively involved in developing new products to individual customer specifications to keep ahead of the competition.

The Company continues to be part of a very successful international organisation supplying their specialised products to over 30 countries, distributed via the groups main warehouses situated at Coventry in the UK and Schaffhausen in Switzerland.

decision to close the foundry was made. The last cast being struck on 28th April 1993 so ending a process so familiar to generations of Bedfordians after 134 years of casting at the old site. The screwed fittings are now produced at the George Fischer plant at Traisen, Austria.

In 1968 another product range, that of Distribution Products to the Gas and Water Industries was developed for use with steel pipes and later for polyethylene pipes. This product range is still being produced at the new factory at Norse Road together with many other products for the gas, water and mechanical industries throughout the world.

The new site has been refurbished to bring it in line with the high standards of George Fischer production techniques and was officially opened on 28th September 1998 by Martin Huber, President of the George Fischer Group. The

Above: *A view of the Norse Road premises today.*
Top: *A 1960s view of the Foundry.*
Below: *The Foundry in the 1980s.*

Better looking through and through

Visitors to Scandinavia and other northern lands used to return home with amazing tales of double windows. When asked by stay-at-homes to describe these and to explain their purpose they replied that there were two windows instead of one. This seemed decidedly odd to their listeners, particularly as, while the outer window opened outwards in the normal fashion, the inner window opened into the room! Suggestions that a system, which effectively insulated wooden houses from temperatures as low as thirty degrees below freezing, might be of use in England were scoffed at.

Since those unbelieving days British manufacturers, such as Kingston Windows, have led the world in the production of one piece double glazing units.

The old style double windows were built with a gap as thick as the walls of the house, anything from around six inches for a log cabin to a foot or so for stone and brick buildings. People regulated the temperature, before the days of controllable central heating, by opening the inner window a little to reduce the insulation value. Russian rooms were equipped with tiny 'winter' windows which could be opened when the main windows were taped shut during the long reign of General Winter.

Fresh air fiends from England, enjoying winter sports holidays, found little alternative between freezing while sleeping with two open windows, or baking in super-heated rooms lacking any ventilation. Such devices and adaptations to winters which lasted for half the year were considered too clumsy for the variable British climate. Early pioneers in British double glazing produced separate glass screens which could be put up inside the main window and as easily unclipped and removed for storage when no longer

Above: Staff in the 1960s. Below: Kingston workers carrying a ladies four rowing boat which was presented to Bedford Rowing Club.

Castle (a name Anglicised from The Infanta of Castile) and the adjacent Leather Bottle, into a workable factory. Here the stock in trade was first hand built to individual order as is still the case for the many buildings equipped with windows in non-standard sizes.

The founder was joined at these Melbourne Street premises by Barrie Francis who has risen to occupy the MD's seat. The 'Swinging Sixties' was the era where the unconventional became the norm and Premier Macmillan told the public 'You've never had it so good'. Part of this heritage was an enormous increase in incomes and living standards which allowed people to whoop it up and invest in bricks and mortar. Double glazing was as much 'in' as Carnaby Street fashions and unlike tastes in music and furnishings double glazing has stayed the course. No one now would dream of building a house without double glazing, or insulation, its companion in energy saving.

needed. These did the job so well that some families have continued to use them having left the screens permanently in place to save the inconvenience of seasonal changes. This style of window fitment became known as secondary glazing.

The next stage in the development of British double glazing systems was the construction of permanently fitted sliding glass secondary glazing screens inside the existing windows which opened outward in the conventional manner. In a way these screens were rather like the famous Yorkshire windows of the 18th and 19th Centuries, which allow ventilation in areas where normal windows are in danger of being blown from their hinges! It is rather fitting that Charles Gallie was inspired by a visit to his glazier cousin in Kingston-upon-Hull, in the East Riding of Yorkshire to enter the new world of double glazing.

From these early days Kingston Windows has pioneered consistently high standards in manufacturing, installation and after care guarantees that have earned national recognition. Since then Kingston Windows has spread its wings from making and fitting windows to designing conservatories tailored to fit customers' houses. The standard range of conservatories offered

Many people thank accidents for a change in their fortunes and Charles Gallie's broken ankle was no exception. Although a printer he decided to learn all he could about double glazing while convalescing in Yorkshire. With the passion of the convert he established his own double glazing business in Bedford, named appropriately enough after the port on the River Hull. In 1964 he converted two redundant pubs, The Elephant and

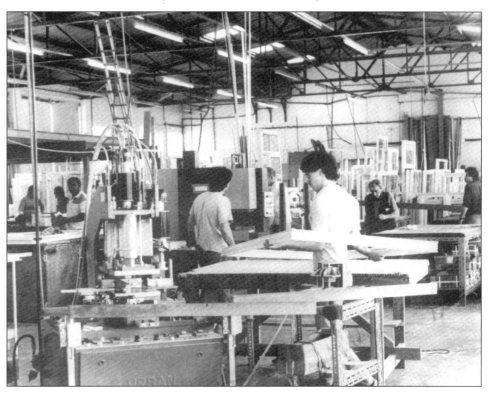

Above: *Kingston replaced all the windows for Perrings, originally Longhurst & Skinner.*
Right: *Staff hard at work in the workshop.*

include Georgian and Victorian styles that would have pleased householders of eras when Orangeries and Winter Gardens were high fashion additions to the homes of a wealthy clientele demanding the most modern technology.

All the work is undertaken by in-house staff trained by the firm to give the highest standard of service to the paying customer. These standards are a hidden benefit to householders who expect to enjoy lower heating bills and a reduction of outside noise from the installation of double glazing. In any area of household supply the wise purchaser looks for firms recommended by previous customers among their acquaintances. 'Cheap jack' cowboys simply do not bother to provide the back-up of staff training and after care service which are built into the Kingston guarantee. Any company that is still going from strength to strength after issuing unequivocal 'Ten Year' Guarantees for nearly forty years has to have a sound customer base of well pleased purchasers.

Both domestic and commercial clients who buy from Kingston will have their purchase installed by Kingston employees rather than some fly-by-night sub contractor. By this means owners of period properties can rely on Kingston to produce goods in keeping with the style and materials of the building. In addition they can be assured that the Kingston craftsmen installing the products will do so in full sympathy for the owner's peace of mind. As many other people entrust work to their own builders Kingston Windows actually provide double glazing products to the trade purchasers who

Top: Just part of the large delivery fleet.
Right: Bedford's Mayoress celebrating Kingston Windows 25th Anniversary.

believe in giving their clients the best available on the wholesale market.

Kingston obtain their raw materials from the Duraflex works in Gloucestershire, the national leader in plastic extrusion of the uPVC used in double glazing window frames. It is after all the quality of the frames which ensure a weather proof fit within the house wall for the two sheets of glass which keep the warmth in and the cold and wet at bay. The actual cutting, shaping and welding of the frames for both standard size and bespoke windows, doors and conservatories is done by Kingston at their Bedford works.

In the last few decades British builders and home owners have reached a stage where no new building is not furnished with double glazing and energy saving insulation. All our citizens can now enjoy home comforts beyond the standards once set by wealthy

Romans, the originators of central heating. The same demand for bodily comfort exists in the commercial world where hoteliers, office based businesses and many other industries recognise that Kingston double glazing saves them money in heat and light bills. In addition clients react well to comfortable conditions in places of business and of refreshment. Beyond that scientific tests show that the all important work force, who cheerfully enter an employer's portals day after day, give their best in comfortable surroundings.

The firm has expanded from its old pub premises to an impressive purpose built factory, called Melbourne House, on Caxton Road. Commercial and trade clients continue to receive a warm welcome at the upgraded original works in Melbourne Street. Domestic customers can view the firm's products at Kingston's showrooms in Bedford and the adjacent former village of Kempston. For those living beyond the immediate Bedford area Kingston has showrooms in Dunstable, Kempston and Conservatory show sites at Willington and Woburn Sands.

As a local firm Kingston plays its part in local life by sponsoring charitable fund raising events such as the Luton swimming day organised by Kingston. This sponsored day raised a total of £4,000 for the Cancer Research Campaign aided by swimmers ranging from absolute beginners to senior citizens who blithely put a mile behind their kicking feet. Local parades and galas frequently enjoy assistance from Kingston whose employees get a kick out of their involvement with friends and neighbours working together for specific community projects, and the company enjoys recognition as large sponsors of local Sports Clubs and Organisations. Kingston recognises the value of commercial liaison with the voluntary sector which is such a vital part of the English way of life.

Top: A craftsman skilfully designing stained glass windows. Below: Conservatories are fast becoming a very popular extension to people's homes.

Power and glory in engineering

As the 20th century draws to a close, we can look back over a tremendous number of innovations and achievements in engineering from which the world has been able to benefit over the course of the century. Closer to home, British citizens can be justifiably proud of Great Britain's contribution to these advances; and, closer still, the people of Bedford can take extra pride in the significant work carried out at the Queen's Engineering Works in the course of the last hundred years.

Now part of Rolls-Royce, the company was first incorporated as W H Allen & Son in 1900 although in fact the Queen's Engineering Works had first been established on this site six years previously. The origins of the firm can be traced back further still, to the founding of the firm of Allen's on a site then adjoining Waterloo Station in York Street, Lambeth, in 1880. Its founder was William Henry Allen. Born in Cardiff in 1844, he had been interested in engineering from an early age and had worked for the London company of J & H Gwynne & Company for 12 years prior to establishing his own works in Lambeth. Gwynne's produced a wide range of centrifugal pumps (trademarked *Invincible*), electric light generating sets, and steam engines to drive them, and so naturally this was the field in which William's own venture was launched. Under the trade name of *Conqueror* he began producing centrifugal pumps for water and sewage applications, for use in land drainage and irrigation scheme, in mines, quarries and large industrial plants, and later for marine applications and dock-pumping schemes; *Conqueror* pumps became known all over the world. A great believer in the value of good training, William had a policy of employing well qualified staff; thus the company was able to keep abreast of the important advances in thermodynamics which came about at the end of the 19th century, when it diversified into the manufacture of forced-draught fans, ventilation fans and condensers.

By this time the firm had been obliged, by the London & South Western Railway Company, to vacate its York Street premises, and William Allen, together with his son Richard who had been taken into partnership in 1890, had after much deliberation selected a 20-acre site on the Queen's Park Estate, on the west side of Bedford. The land was duly purchased from the Whitbread family; a large proportion of the York Street workforce opted to move with the firm, and Allen's commenced production in Bedford in 1894.

Above: *WH Allen, founder of the company.*
Below: *The 1918 visit of King George V and Queen Mary to Queen's Engineering Works.*

fans driven by reciprocating steam engines and steam turbines were used on the great liners of the first decades of the 20th century, including the giant Cunard liners, and White Star's Olympic and Titanic. During the first world war, by which time the firm's reputation as the leading British manufacturer of marine auxiliary machinery was firmly established, the British fleet relied heavily on Allen machinery. Items manufactured for the Admiralty at Queen's Engineering Works included 16 sets of geared steam turbines for patrol boats, two cruising turbines for destroyers, steam turbine-driven salvage pumps and various engines for minesweepers, trawlers, launches and pinnaces. In some cases the items they were called upon to produce required considerable innovation and ingenuity; and this was the case once more in the second world war, when orders from the Admiralty included, in addition to the more conventional items, ten sets of specially designed steam turbines and condensers to drive hydraulic pumps to operate the big guns on the King George V class battleships.

From that date on the company was to remain in the hands of William Allen and his descendants for more than 75 years, during which period both the company and the individual members of this remarkable family won great respect worldwide for their work. It is impossible to list the many achievements with which the Allen name has been associated over the years. Of particular note must be the company's role, through its connection with Ferranti, in the early development of electric light generating machinery; its contribution to shipbuilding; and its pioneering work in the manufacture of diesel and aero engines. Richard Allen received a knighthood in 1942 for his services to the Royal Navy; Kenneth Allen received a knighthood in 1961 in recognition of his services to engineering and to British trade and industry.

The manufacture of aero engines was another area in which Queen's Engineering Works made an important contribution to the country's defences during the first world war. Again, this was a completely new venture for the company. It produced its first Le Rhone air-cooled rotary engine in March 1916, and proceeded to supply a total of 3,221 engines between then and the end of the war; these were installed in DH5, Sopwith Scout, Bristol Scout and Avro aircraft.

Turbine production commenced at Queen's Engineering Works in 1908, and Allen electric generators, pumps and

Above: *A 1950s view of the Queen's Engineering Works.*
Top: *A regular sight on Bedford roads was this low-loader, used to transport the finished products.*

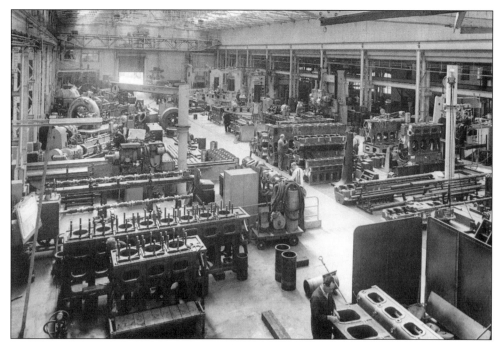

Limited, was formed. This company then became part of Rolls-Royce in 1989, and has derived from this association a greater security and stability which will enable it to remain at the very forefront of modern technology, and continue the tradition of engineering excellence with which this remarkable company has been synonymous for more than a century.

Focusing solely on diesels, today Rolls-Royce at the Queen's Engineering Works has reduced its response times to customer enquiries by introducing the latest information technology systems and, of course, by developing its international network of overseas service centres and representation. An essential feature of the modern international power project is the ability to secure funding. The company has therefore worked hard to make financial support another element of its customer support package. The diesel business within the Rolls-Royce group can draw on the company knowledge and resources together with its extensive contacts in the world financial community. This means that financial packages can be arranged with ease and can vary from straightforward loans to build, own and operate arrangements.

With all this in mind, coupled with the ongoing multi-million pound investment programme into the modernisation and upgrading of its production facilities, Rolls-Royce looks set to become a major player in the international supply of diesel power plants for many years to come.

Top: A 1960s view of the diesel engine erecting shop.
Above left: The launch of the Allen 5000 series engine in March 1998.

Meanwhile, preliminary work on the manufacture of the internal combustion engine had begun in 1906; petrol/paraffin oil engines and air-blast diesel engines were developed, and a prototype gas engine, designed and patented by Hugh Fullagar, was built. In 1912 the company obtained a licence to manufacture diesel engines. Diesel engines have, of course, remained one of the company's great strengths. Subsequent key developments in this area include the introduction of the airless injection diesel engine in 1928 and its application, from 1933 onwards, in ship propulsion and in railway locomotives; the introduction of turbo-charging in 1956, which increased the power output by up to 50 per cent and was before long applied to all types of diesel engine; and the introduction of intercooling in 1962, another design breakthrough which greatly added to the power output of the engine. Today, Allen diesel engines are in great demand throughout the world for use in power stations and for all manner of pumping and industrial applications; and with the company now operating under the Rolls-Royce banner, customers are assured of the best technical advice and support.

In the latter half of the 20th century a series of organisational changes proved necessary in order to maintain its position in a changing industrial climate. Having acquired William Foster & Company of Lincoln in 1960 and their subsidiary Gwynne Pumps, the company merged with Belliss & Morcom of Birmingham in 1968 and a new company, Amalgamated Power Engineering Company

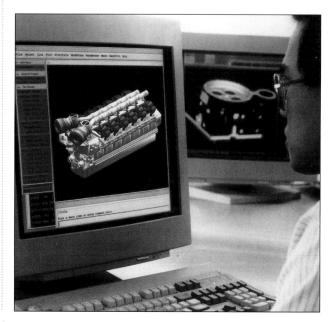

Bedfordia - big business with a christian outlook

The entrepreneurial spirit responsible for creating the business empire which operates today as the Bedfordia Group has been active for almost three-quarters of a century, and throughout the whole of that period the business has been run by the Ibbett family. Three generations have contributed to the growth and success of the organisation through their own particular ideas, interests and skills, while the family's sincere commitment to the Christian faith is consistently reflected in all the Group's undertakings. The current Chief Executive of the Group is John Ibbett, who took over from his father Clifton in 1993; and it was Clifton Ibbett's father, Claude Valentine Ibbett, whose imagination and enterprise launched the business that was to be the first step in the formation of the Bedfordia Group.

Claude's very first business venture, which he ran in partnership with his brother, consisted chiefly of selling pianos and wireless sets. This venture was set up in 1930, prior to which Claude had worked for his father's drapery business in Kempston; it was an era when both pianoforte and wireless played a central role in family life, and the Ibbett brothers' business was a success.

From small beginnings grew — Bedfordia

A TOP company boss handed a bouquet to his staff when he and 300 guests met at Bedford's Moat House to celebrate 40 years of Bedfordia.

Mr Clifton Ibbett, managing director of the Oakley-based Bedfordia group and its sister London City and Metropolitan Property Group, told his guests at the 40th anniversary luncheon: "I put a large part of our success down to the quality, loyalty and endeavour of our staff.

"Our company is very fortunate to have a staff which has always made a point of putting a great deal of effort into making the business a success."

Mr Ibbett, son of the founder and present chairman of the Bedfordia operation, Mr Claude Ibbett, was speaking to an audience of guests drawn from industry, commerce, trade unions and local authorities from all over Britain.

He paid a tribute to his father when he told guests: "We are here today because my father laid some solid foundations when he started out by forming a building company to the point here today we employ 40 staff."

The Bedfordia group mushroomed out of a farming enterprise formed in 1939 which now farms more than 2,800 acres. The company has taken over house building, sand and gravel plants, box and carton manufacturers, farm equipment, trailers and transporters and even a summer holiday firm.

So extensive is the group's operation that recently a firm in the group, Presletta of Southport, was asked to design a special "logo" for the Queen's Flight.

At the luncheon staff had a surprise in store for group chairman, Mr Claude Ibbett, when they presented him with a silver rosebowl.

Perhaps one of the most spectacular aspects of the Bedfordia operation has been the growth of Courtburn Ltd, a company formed to cater for the machine tool and welding field. From small beginnings Courtburn now operates from new factory and offices covering 35,000 square feet in Windsor Road, Bedford.

Courtburn was the site for a VIP visit prior to the lunch when mineworkers' union leader, Mr Joe Gormley, was among a large party of guests who visited the factory.

Mr Gormley was particularly interested to see a newly imported machine which Courtburn engineers have adapted for use in mine safety and rescue.

Joe Gormley with Mr Claude Ibbett.

In 1935 Claude's entrepreneurial spirit took a new direction: housebuilding. There was a growing need for new houses in the area, and Claude set about meeting that need, establishing the building company Besbuilt two years later and going on to construct a large number of good-quality, reasonably-priced houses on the outskirts of Bedford. The company's operations were then disrupted by the coming of war and the resulting shortage of both labour and materials. In 1939 Claude, who had started looking into the possibility of gravel extraction, took up a lease on a farm in Milton Ernest with a view to extracting gravel from the land under a royalty agreement with the owner. In the event this proved uneconomic as there was

Above left: *Bedfordia celebrated its 40th anniversary in 1979.* ***Below:*** *Bedfordia Grain Services' 27,000 tonne capacity grain silos at Milton Ernest.*

insufficient gravel there, but Claude continued to manage the farm, and subsequently formed a partnership with Colin McKie. Together the two men farmed a growing acreage for 17 years, during which time their herds of high-yielding Friesian and Ayrshire cows and Large White pigs became famous.

As supplies returned to normal after the war Besbuilt resumed operations, and in due course a renewal of his interest in gravel prompted Claude to found Welford Gravels. This developed into a thriving concern., with gravel pits in Essex, Bedfordshire, Northamptonshire, Lancashire and Cumbria supplying large quantities of the building materials used in various national construction programmes including the motorway projects which were a feature of the 60s. In due course the business was disposed of when large-scale programmes of this nature came to an end.

In 1953 Claude's son Clifton left school and began work as a farmhand; the life suited him and four years later he took on some 200 acres and began farming on his own account. This marked the beginning of Bedfordia Farms. By 1961 Clifton had taken over the original farm of Ibbett and McKie, merging it with his own, and today those original 200 acres have grown into 5,500 acres, with a dairy herd of around 300 cows and 200 followers, and a pig herd of 900 sows and 4,000 growers. There has been

This page: *Examples of equipment hired out by Bedfordia Plant.*

a very marked growth in the farming business since it was taken over by John Ibbett in the mid 80s.

Meanwhile Clifton had begun to take an active interest in property investment and development, and during the 1960s he was involved in a succession of business ventures, all of which were subsequently sold on by the family as thriving concerns, with the capital being re-invested in new enterprises. Among the assorted companies which he took over, built up and sold on during this period were Raymond Cook Travel, the specialist engineering firm Courtburn, a printing company, and an agricultural business which sold tractors and other farm machinery; Bedfordia Plant, started by Clifton in 1963, grew to be the largest regional plant hire company in the south east and subsequently extended into Scotland and the Shetland

Isles where it supplied a great deal of equipment for the growing oil industry. By the time it was sold in 1980 this very successful business was operating from 16 separate depots. Meanwhile, in 1979 Clifton had set up a firm which has remained an important part of the family business; Bedfordia Motor Holdings currently operates three franchised dealerships - BMW, Chrysler Jeep and Daihatsu - at separate premises, with the BMW and Chrysler dealerships recently installed in new, multi-million pound flagship sites on the edge of town.

Of the many and varied ventures in which the Group has been involved over the years, some of which have been mentioned above, it is perhaps farming which, always one of the Group's principle activities, has been one of the greatest sources of pleasure for both Clifton and his son John. Today, the efficiency of Bedfordia Farms means that even in these difficult times they are able to maintain a steady profit margin, and it is not uncommon for farmers to approach Bedfordia with a view to farming under a cost-share, profit-share agreement.

Nineteen seventy-nine was also the year in which the Bedfordia Group marked its 40th anniversary with a celebratory luncheon in Bedford, and a large number of business associates and friends joined the family and their employees in looking back over the many successes and achievements of the first 40 years. The 20 years since that event have seen a continual growth in the catalogue of successful under-takings and the number of customers and suppliers whose respect goodwill has been earned by the Group in its various activities; and the Group's success story will continue long into the future.

The Bedfordia Group of companies is a remarkable organisation. The Group's pursuit of its interests in farming, construction, transport and leisure have done much to enhance the quality of life for the inhabitants of Bedford and beyond, as through the skill, determination and enterprise of its leaders it has played an increas-ingly important role in the economic devel-opment of the region. At the same time the environment has benefited from the Bedfordia Group's commitment to conservation and preservation of the beauty of our surroundings. Above all, throughout its success the Group

In recent years the Group has concentrated its activ-ities on farming, property investment and devel-opment and car retailing. Separate companies have been set up to focus on the different aspects of farming: arable, dairy and grassland farming; grain analysis, processing and storage; and pig breeding and rearing. The Group has accumulated a very substantial property portfolio, and this is maintained and admin-istered by the Property and Development companies which also identify potential land development oppor-tunities. The Group has also set up a specialist finance house.

has continued to operate according to the strong Christian values of its founder and his descendants; in all aspects of its business, equal emphasis is placed on ethics, profession-alism, sustainability and profitability. Everyone who has dealings with the Bedfordia Group in its 60 years of existence have come to appreciate the honesty, fairness, compassion and respect for the individual which charac-terise all the Group's dealings; and we can all take heart from this living proof that in this day and age, big business can still operate so successfully on Christian principals.

Above: Bedfordia's sponsorship of a roundabout was marked by a visit from the Mayor, who is seen here sitting astride the Bedford Sheep - Bedford's answer to Milton Keynes' Stone Cows.

Making life easier for the motorist after a shattering experience

Anyone who has ever had their windscreen shattered by a stone whilst driving at speed, or gone out to their car in the morning to find a smashed window and the stereo gone, will know what a sickening feeling of frustration and helplessness the sight of all those bits of fractured glass can conjure up in the pit of the stomach. But the lucky ones will discover that the problem can be easily solved by one telephone call to Autoglass.

Indeed, 'making life easier for the customer' is part of Autoglass' central philosophy - which is refreshing in a company with a nationwide network of around 180 branches and approaching 900 mobile service units, and can perhaps be attributed to its origins as a small family concern based in Bedford. Simply called Windshields, it was started by Tony Bates in 1969, at premises in Dean Street which were to remain home to the firm until 1980. A number of ex-GPO Morris 1000 vans were acquired and used as service vehicles; readers might remember that Morris 1000s of that era were fitted with front wings made of rubber, which offered many practical advantages for the driver prone to minor bumps. At that time, too, toughened glass was used for vehicle windscreens. Unlike the laminated screens (which have been in common use for the last decade or so) a toughened

windscreen will smash when struck with sufficient force, and the offending object is likely to end up on the driver's lap. In fact the grit with which the highways of East Anglia and Suffolk were regularly resurfaced often proved too much for toughened screens.

Below: Autoglass not only repair car windscreens - as this 1980s picture shows.
Bottom: The control room in the 1980s.

Windshields and Autoglass merged in 1984 to become Autoglass Windshields. A year later the word Windshields was dropped and the name Autoglass remains to this day. Prior to this Windshields had already left its original premises at Dean Street, moving in 1980 to Kingsway House in Kingsway; the company subsequently moved out when its Cardington Road workshop site was redeveloped to include office accommodation. It then moved back into Kingsway House for another spell before relocating to Clifton House, and then finally from there to its current home at the fantastic, purpose-built building at Priory Business Park, Cardington, in 1997. Dominated by a huge glass curved roof (rather like a windscreen) and overlooking a lake, the company has come a long way from the first tiny office!

Customer satisfaction has always been the company's priority, and every possible innovation is adopted to make life easier for the motorist. One such innovation was the introduction of the Autoglass Call Centre 17 years ago, as a move towards improved customer service. Centralised call handling was at that time a novel solution to the challenge of providing an initial point of contact for a growing number of customers spread over a wide geographical area. The value of this dedicated call-handling facility in dealing attentively and efficiently with customers' requests soon became evident, and the role of the Call Centre has become central to the entire operation. From small beginnings - in a portakabin, which was originally a coffin makers, with four seats and no technology beyond a 'key and lamp' telephone system - the Call Centre has continued to grow, keeping pace with an increasing number of customers whose expectations are constantly rising. Today the Call Centre has 64 seats and employs 159 Customer Advisers who handle 1.6 million calls per year, operating 24 hours a day, seven days a week, 365 days a year. The introduction of leading edge technology has been a key factor contributing to the outstanding performance of the Call Centre. Equipped with the latest Computer and Telephony Integrated technology (CTI), operators have at their fingertips all the technical data and up-to-date information necessary to respond to each call swiftly and efficiently. Because CTI makes it easy to handle every situation correctly without prior expert knowledge and complex technical training, operators can be

Top: *The company's second premises at Cardington Road, Bedford, which is now the Bedford branch.*
Above left: *Control room technology in the 1980s.*

selected on the basis of their inter-personal or 'people-orien-tated' skills, and this ensures that customers are always greeted and dealt with in a friendly and competent way which equals their highest expectations.

Just as the application of improved communication and information technology has made it possible for customers to enjoy unprecedented levels of customer service, so windscreen repair techniques themselves have become much more sophisticated over the years. Today's motorists take for granted the fast-bonding adhesives which mean they can drive off as soon as windscreen replacement has been carried out, and the technology which gives them the option of having minor damage repaired, saving them the expense of buying a complete new screen (Autoglass, incidentally, pioneered both these developments).

Meanwhile, the rise in car crime has changed the nature of Autoglass' business significantly in the last decade or so. In the days of the rubber-winged Morris 1000s virtually all glass breakages were caused by accidental damage, but these days motorists who are victims of vandalism and theft account for a significant proportion of customers. To try and combat this trend, Autoglass carries out an in-depth analysis into car crime, and works with Crime Concern in running the 'Cracking Car Crime' campaign which is designed to show motorists what steps they can take to protect themselves against car crime, while throughout the year all Autoglass branches offer windscreen security etchings as part of the initiative to beat car thieves.

Road safety is a primary consideration of the windscreen replacement and repair industry, and Autoglass' commitment to this cause goes far beyond its day-to-day business activities. The company had a tradition for leading campaigns on issues connected with driver safety both locally and nationally, and indeed it has gained a number of awards for its efforts in this area and won respect from many sectors of the community.

Another group of people who greatly appreciate Autoglass' peripheral activities in a different sphere are the supporters of Chelsea Football Club - at the time of writing, Autoglass is approaching the end of its second year of a four-year sponsorship deal, and supporters of the Blues living in Bedford will be looking forward to seeing Autoglass' continued support help their team on to even greater success next season.

With 24-hour service, a memorable 0800 36 36 36 freephone number and guaranteed fast response, it is hard to see how service standards can be improved upon; but Autoglass will not rest on its laurels - it will strive to maintain customer service excellence and will continue working to ensure that motorists enjoy the safest possible motoring conditions as they drive into the 21st century.

AUTOGLASS®

Below (both pictures): *Autoglass today.*

Well brewed at the sign of the Eagle

Charles Wells was born in Bedford in 1842. At the young age of fourteen he left school and embarked on a maritime career which was later to be brought to an abrupt end. His first ocean going experience was on the *Devonshire,* a frigate which sailed to India and one of his longest trips took him around the Cape of Good Hope to Australia.

In the 1860s Charles asked his childhood sweetheart, Miss Josephine Grimbley to marry him, however Miss Grimbley's father demanded that Charles abandon his maritime career first. Under no circumstances was Josephine to be left alone for long periods of time while Charles was at sea. Charles relented and made the somewhat unusual move from sea captain to brewer after purchasing a brewery at Horne Lane in Bedford in 1876. Competition in Bedford was fierce with four other breweries pursuing aggressive expansion policies but Charles, who was known for his frankness and honesty, proved to be a shrewd businessman and established his brewery as the dominant player.

After Charles retired, his three eldest sons, Charles Ernest, George Hayward and Sidney Richard ran the brewery in turn. Richard went on to have nine children, two of whom David and Oliver, succeeded each other as Chairmen. The next Chairman was John who retired in 1998 and Paul took over as Managing Director. Tom Wells was appointed Vice-Chairman in 1998. The youngest member of the family to work for the brewery is Peter, Charles' great-great grandson who joined the company as a Trade Marketing Manager in 1997.

In 1976, the year of its centenary, the brewery moved from its original Horne Lane site to a new, purpose built site, the Eagle Brewery. However the water used in Charles Wells' beer is still drawn from the original well sunk over a century ago.

Today the Charles Wells brewery is the largest independent family brewery in Great Britain. The brewery has an estate of over 250 pubs in England and 50 in Europe and is also part owner of the two major music venues in London; The Shepherds Bush Empire and Brixton Academy. Charles Wells also exports its portfolio of beers to more than 30 countries worldwide. The brewery's commitment to and excellence within the export market led to them being

Above: *Charles Wells.*
Below: *The transport fleet c1920.*

awarded the prestigious Queen's Award for Export Achievement in 1997.

Charles Wells brands are known and loved worldwide. The brewery has a long standing passion for real ale and is dedicated to preserving and continuing the tradition of cask and real ale. One of Charles Wells' cask seasonal ales has been brewed in memory of the woman behind the brewery; Josephine Grimbley. This refreshing ale is available during springtime across the Charles Wells estate and free trade outlets. Other seasonal ales include Golden Summer Solstice and Festival Gold.

The most popular and recognisable of Charles Wells cask ales is Bombardier English Premium Bitter. Bombardier English Premium Bitter (4.3%ABV) is an award winning traditional English Ale which is noted for its distinctive copper colour. Its characteristic robust flavour is derived from the finest barley malt, famous Challenger and Golding hops and, not least that, unique 'something' arising from the use of water drawn from the brewery's own well. The English guild of Beer Writers beer writer of the year 1999, Alastair Gilmour, describes the ale as *"The definitive English Bitter whose unexpectedly light, fruity flavour*

and mere suggestion of malt settles on the palate after a lap of honour over every curve of the tongue."

Within Bedfordshire, Charles Wells favourite cask ale is the majestic Eagle IPA (3.6% ABV) which has been brewed to an age old recipe that has been carefully protected by five generations of the Wells family. Like many who sample this ale, Alastair Gilmour fell in love with the distinct flavour. He refers to Eagle as having *"An aroma of freshly sliced apples. Its amber hue is emphasised by a tight, rich head, setting it up as an ale with real credentials. A touch of caramel sweetness is embraced by a slow build up of dryness with all the patience of a string section anticipating the conductor's baton".*

Charles Wells has a passion for beer which embraces all kinds of beers, including lager. The brewery is unique in that it has three foreign lagers within its portfolio; Kirin from Japan, Red Stripe from Jamaica and Corona from Mexico. Kirin and Red Stripe are both brewed in Bedford under licence in the UK by Charles Wells.

Above: *One of the dray wagons at the turn of the 20th century.*
Top: *An early view of the Eagle Brewery.*

Kirin is one of the biggest selling beer brands worldwide and Charles Wells are only one of 4 breweries who have been given the much sought after licence to brew Kirin. Kirin is brewed in Bedford to the original recipe by a UK based Japanese Master Brewer and this thus ensures that Kirin is the freshest possible oriental premium lager in bars and restaurants across the country.

Red Stripe has been brewed under licence in Bedford since 1976. The beer was first brewed in Jamaica over 60 years ago, and Charles Wells continues to use only imported yeast and hops from Washington State's Yakima Valley. Red Stripe's eye catching branding can be seen on bottles, cans and on draught in bars across UK and Europe. Its streetwise and stylish image and

distinctive flavour has led Red Stripe to become one of Europe's fastest growing beer brands.

Charles Wells is a company well respected both at home and abroad. The company is known for the consistently high quality of its beers as well as its innovative approach to dispensing beer. The brewery has recently launched a shaped can into the UK ale market. The can is designed to be eye-catching and tactile and to stand out from the usual cans on the supermarket shelf. Charles Wells also patented the first illuminated drip tray and font. With this unique dispense method, drinkers can clearly see the beer they are buying. The beer is illuminated as it is dispensed into the glass which highlights the theatre and spectacle of the swirling colours and textures of the beer.

The latest in a long line of innovations is a table top beer tap which is controlled by the drinker. One-third of a pint of Kirin is poured from a tap at the touch of a button into glasses provided in a compartment set into each table. An automatic teller, fitted next to the beer tap, accounts for the amount drunk and presents the customer with the total at the end of each evening. This innovation is currently available in Yo! Below, a bar in Soho, London. Both Charles Wells and Yo! Below plan to roll out this mechanism nationwide.

Charles Wells is committed to producing a consistency and high quality of beer which acknowledges and embraces the traditional craftsmanship of brewing while at the same time welcomes an ongoing policy of investment which ensures that the brewery is equipped with the latest technology in beer production. Charles Wells have a true English family passion for beer.

Left: *A pub sign which depicts the Blackwall frigate Kent, on which the founder served.*
Below: *One of the Brewery's inns.*

The goldmine in the High Street

Stepping inside Goldings on the High Street is like stepping back in time. The shop is crammed with pots, pans and other items of household hardware, and the whiff of paraffin is a reminder of the days when every shop had its own distinctive smell - antiseptic in the chemist, leather in the shoe shop, and freshly-baked bread at the baker. Nowadays Goldings also stocks all the latest DIY products as well, of course, but the emphasis is definitely on traditional, quality, well-crafted goods made to last a lifetime.

The people of Bedford have been buying their hardware from Goldings for well over a century. It was in 1867 that the original Mr Golding bought up the existing ironmonger's business of William Day & Son at 80 High Street; Day's was one of around a dozen ironmongers scattered across Bedford, along with Kilpin & Bills, Page, Bacchus, Randalls, Newman, Woodford, Sauce and other local household names of the era. Although unfortunately we have no exact record of the date on which Mr Golding moved across the road from number 80 to number 107, contemporary documents show that the move must have taken place between 1898 and 1901; so at the time of writing we must be very close to the business's centenary at that address.

Left: *An interior view of the shop.*
Below: *The premises in the 1960s.*

About that time, too, the business changed hands. It was bought by Mr Rigby-Smith of Russell Avenue, Bedford, at the turn of the 20th century, who in turn sold it to Samuel Flower in 1919. Unfortunately, Samuel Flower's health began to deteriorate; he began to rely increasingly on his staff to help him with the moving the heavy stock around and share the responsibility of running the business with him, but was let down badly. However, in 1925 his problem was solved. One of the commercial travellers with whom Mr Flower dealt knew that the assistant who worked at Newman's ironmongers in Kingston-on-Thames was origi-

Duke Street, but he did not enjoy it. He stuck it for a year, then he was taken on as an apprentice by Randalls in St Mary's Street; they sent him to evening class twice a week to learn a variety of useful skills such as book-keeping, sign writing, plumbing and lathe operating, and Ernest thoroughly enjoyed his apprenticeship. Unfortunately at the end of his term of apprenticeship Randalls had no permanent vacancy to offer him, but they gave him an excellent reference and he got a good job as a junior assistant, with an excellent salary of £5 a week, at Newman's in Kingston-on-Thames. He had been working there for a year when his mother fell ill and he felt that he ought to return to Bedford; so when he heard, via the commercial traveller, that the owner of Goldings in Bedford was looking for a manager, he was immediately interested. Mr Flower could offer him only £2.15s.0d a week, which was a considerable drop in salary, but Ernest decided that as he would be living at home he could afford to accept it, and returned to Bedford to begin what was to be a successful and long-term association with Goldings.

Goldings' customers may remember that in 1992, when the shop celebrated the 125th anniversary of the beginning of the business, Ernest Lain was still very active, carrying out his duties as Company Secretary at the age of 89. Out of the many ironmongers which existed in Bedford when Goldings was founded, Goldings is the only one which has survived, preserving the values of the family business and stocking a vast range of the quality hardware products which continue to give good service to every generation. The traditional nature of the business seems to attract loyal staff; Mrs Ellen Deeley (Scottie) and Vic Warner are just two of the firm's long-serving employees whom customers got to know well over the years. Vic Warner was taken on as an apprentice and is now one of the directors, along with Tony Lain, Ernest's son.

A hundred years at number 107; 132 years in business; 75 years since the Lain family joined the business - Goldings has a lot to celebrate. We wish them every success in the future.

nally from Bedford and wanted to return home to be near his mother, who was in poor health. This young man was Ernest Lain. His parents, Albert and Annie Lain, had been living in Hurst Grove when Ernest was born but had subsequently moved to Rutland Road. Albert, a commercial traveller, wanted to make sure that his children had settled careers, and when Ernest, who was the middle of their five children, decided at the age of fifteen that he wanted to be a concert pianist, his father urged him to keep music as a hobby and learn a trade. So Ernest became an office boy at Harry Ball's, the auctioneers on the corner of Mill Street and

Above left: *A recent view of Goldings' premises.*
Top: *Part of the company's 125 year celebrations was a competition to guess the number of lines it has in stock. Ernest Lain is seen here with the winners.*

The Solicitors who care, since 1809

Although the partnership name of Sharman and Trethewy was adopted in 1892 the legal practice was originally established by Francis John Budd in 1809. He worked from St Paul's Square as Attorney-at-Law and Solicitor in the Court of Chancery. In 1831 on the death of Francis John Budd, a year before the Great Reform Act, which gave the vote to respectable copyholders renting property worth £10 a year, Alexander Sharman acquired the practice. Alexander Sharman then practiced alone between 1831-38 in Bedford, before taking on John Budd's son-in-law, Thomas Wesley Turnley, as his partner.

Following Alexander Sharman's death in 1853, Thomas Wesley Turnley in 1855, the second year of the Crimean War, took in Mark Sharman, Alexander Sharman's son, as his partner. The next stage in the development of this family practice was when William Smail became the third partner in 1868 up until Thomas Wesley Turnley died in 1875. It was then common for all to work until they dropped in harness, either from dire need or because idleness held no charms. The business then became known as Sharman and Smail up until 1889, when Mark Sharman ran it on his own for some three years both as a Solicitor and Commissioner for Oaths.

The present name of the firm was adopted when a Cornishman, Alfred Tresawna Trethewy, joined Mark Sharman as partner in 1892; he practiced until 1929, outliving his senior partner by sixteen years. The Sharman connection continued until 1918 when Frederic Sharman, son of Mark Sharman, died after having joined the firm in 1896. The firm continued in this way under the direction of eight further partners, joining and leaving in overlapping sequence, until the end of 1973 when it incorporated the practice of Tebbs and Son on New Year's Day, 1974.

It has been a long standing tradition of the firm that the partners in their spare time play a valuable part in the social and charitable organisations of the town and the county. Local schools and different sports and other clubs have benefited from the freely given expertise of partners, which has been offered since Alexander

Above: *Alexander Sharman.*
Below: *88 Dunstable Street, Ampthill (the offices of Sharman & Trethewy since 1925).*

Sharman's connections with the Bedford and Leicester Railway and politics in the 1840s. He later became Mayor of Bedford while Thomas Wesley Turnley was Secretary to the Bedfordshire Agricultural Society which spread the gospel of modern farming long before the foundation of modern agricultural colleges. Other organisations which have benefited and still benefit include local Councils, the local Chambers of Trade and Rotary and other Clubs.

For several generations in the 19th century the Liberal Party was served by partners acting as local Agents. Ampthill UDC was served with the same generosity of time, which reflects the willingness to serve others, which is so vital a part of public life in England. It follows that those who willingly give time to good works will provide their clients with a standard of service dedicated to serving their clients' interests. As a firm Sharman and Trethewy provides a combination of legal expertise and accumulated knowledge and experience which serves its clients well. It is not surprising that clients turn to the firm from one generation to the next for professional assistance in their legal and financial affairs.

Several of the Partners are also Notaries. All the firm's Notaries are legally authorised to authenticate documents for use abroad. Such qualification is recognised by countries and courts throughout the world. The firm utilises the latest IT (Information Technology) to assist in providing cost effective, efficient and proactive legal services. As a member of the Agricultural

Law Association, the practice is also able to look after the interests of farming clients. Since 1988 the firm has been a founder member of the Solicitors Information Group (SIG). The firm is accredited as an 'Investor in People' and is also a Legal Aid franchise holder, offering justice to all regardless of wealth.

The Partners are justly proud of their long history of practicing in St Paul's Square and Harpur Street, Bedford and Dunstable Street, Ampthill and the part they have played and continue to play in the fabric of Bedford and Bedfordshire.

Above: *1 Harpur Street, Bedford, (The offices of Sharman & Trethewy since 1899).*
Below: *The Partners of 1999.*

Reddings Wood, Ampthill - home of Hunting Engineering

Hunting Engineering began life in 1957 but one has to look further back to find the seed from which the company grew. It began in 1950 as a small Research Department within Percival Aircraft - a member of the Hunting Group of companies - based at Luton Airport. The department was formed in order to design, develop and manufacture components for the new breed of post-war weapons, and a close working relationship with government establishments and agencies evolved. The department became highly regarded by the customer and, as a result, received more work and wider responsibilities.

By 1957 the department had grown into a division and became a separate company entitled Hunting Engineering Limited in that year. The new company was a subsidiary of Hunting Aircraft Company (as Percival Aircraft had become known) and the first Chairman was Sir Percy Hunting. Hunting Engineering continued to conduct business at Luton Airport until Hunting Aircraft Company was taken over in 1961 by the British Aircraft Corporation. It became necessary

Above: Charles Hunting, founder of the Hunting Group.
Below: The site in the 1970s.

at that time for Hunting Engineering, which remained within the Hunting Group to find new premises. The company had already taken a lease on the former Bovril factory at Reddings Wood, Ampthill and was using it for overflow work of a non-classified nature. It was decided that the Ampthill site had all the development potential required and in 1962 work commenced on a new office building. The new building was occupied at the end of 1962, by which time the company was rapidly expanding and a second building phase was already being planned. Until the completion of the second phase, the company personnel were split between Reddings Wood and Luton.

Two other companies occupied adjacent premises at Ampthill, one being Bovril which still used a building on the site and Ferguson, the last maker of Ebonite in the UK. By 1978 Hunting Engineering had acquired the premises of the two neighbouring companies. The Hunting site then extended to 70 acres, including a sports field of 15 acres and a good deal of natural woodland. The company gave much thought to the preservation of the amenities of the site and the result is a happy marriage of countryside and industry. This approach has led to excellent relationships with the Planning Authority and the local community. Research into the history of the area has revealed that Reddings Wood has been a natural woodland for many centuries and old maps in County Records Office show it had much the same outline in the 16th century as it has now.

Apart from some limited excursions into other design and development work, Hunting Engineering has concentrated

on defence projects. The company has played a major part in every nuclear weapon development project, the most recent being Chevaline, the updating of the Polaris strategic deterrent. In the mid 60s the company entered into the field of conventional airborne weapons when a contract to design and develop a retarding tail for conventional High Explosive bombs was secured. The expansion of the business into land based and seaborne weapons soon followed.

Over the years the company has developed greatly, providing not only a comprehensive design and development service, but also the ability and resources to plan and fulfil large production contracts. The company's workforce includes highly qualified systems engineers specialising in mathematics, physics, aerodynamics and other sciences as well as mechanical, electrical and control engineering. In 1993, Hunting Communications Technology Limited, a sister company based on the south coast of England, moved to Ampthill and became the Communications Division of Hunting Engineering. This move further expanded the business interests of the company to include military communi-

cations equipment, providing a complete design, development and production service for installations, military shelters and field generators. The Division is the UK Ministry of Defence Design Authority for CIS installations into all armoured vehicles and a wide range of other vehicles.

The company today employs around 750 staff and successfully collaborates with many large international defence companies in what is now a highly competitive defence industry. As one of the largest employers in the area, Hunting Engineering is of some importance to the local community. The company has always been amenable to the use of its facilities by the local organisations and charities and continues to seek new ways to support the area whenever possible.

Above: *One of the company's products - the BL755.*
Top: *The main executive offices at Reddings Wood, opened in 1978 by the Secretary of State for Defence.*
Below: *Reddings Wood today showing the new buildings on the Upper Lawn site.*

The Hinckleys, a Horticultural family

Few people make drastic career changes that take them from the relatively safe ranks of the employed and into the risky and challenging business of being one's own boss. Such a merchant venturer was Ronald Hinckley, the son of James Hinckley, a bookkeeper who supplemented his income by growing and selling vegetables and flowers from his allotment garden door to door using a hand made cart. The early death of James in 1955 prevented him from achieving his dream which was brought to fruition by son Ronald, founder of J Hinckley and Sons.

Ron Hinckley, having been brought up by a skilled gardener, knew what he was doing when he gave up his job as a clothing salesman in 1953 to buy a plot of land in Caves Lane. At the time this contained a number of fruit trees and he cared for these and, in season, sold the apples, pears and plums. An attempt was made at keeping poultry but was found to be unprofitable on such a small scale. A small dilapidated greenhouse existed on the land and so it was decided to grow bedding plants and, when filled, held 70 trays. These, and all other produce, from the smallholding were sold at the twice weekly Bedford Market where Ron's mother, Selina, and later Ron's wife Doreen worked on the family stall. Those days followed the ancient tradition of producer selling direct to the customer which was devilish hard work for limited rewards. Brother Raymond joined Ron in 1956 to provide another strong back for the growing company and another greenhouse, a Duncan Tucker was built.

Nursery work in the 1950s and 60s still depended on hand tools and muscle power to cultivate the local clay soils. The first mechanical aid to join the firm was a petrol driven Rotavator and opened up the facility to start producing outdoor crops during the spring and summer months. The fierce winter of 1962, when farmers used pneumatic drills to lift root crops, devastated production so much that the Hinckleys were absent from Bedford Market for several weeks, a disaster that nearly broke a business with low cash reserves.

The company moved to larger premises at Great Barford in 1962 and the land at Caves Lane was later sold for building purposes in the early 70s. They further expanded in 1990 by the purchase of a second nursery at Wyboston. By 1964 Hinckleys purchased their first van for £477. Accounts were still done

Above left: *James Hinckley, the founder of the company.* ***Below:*** *The Cave Lane premises in 1964.*

carefully by hand and it was not until Ron's sons entered the business in 1982 that these were first computerised in 1988. The 1980s saw massive expansion including the purchase of the first tractor, more glasshouses, a coldroom and the decision to leave Bedford Market after thirty two years on the same stall. The firm continued to grow flowers for direct sales to florist shops within a sixty mile radius of Bedford and to wholesalers throughout Britain.

as much as the service which goes with it. The Hinckleys are, indeed, a prize winning family of horticulturists and, one which their founder, James Hinckley, would have been proud.

Above: The market stall in 1964.
Below: David, Ron and John Hinckley with 'Alaska', the award-winning lily produced by the company.

J Hinckley and Sons were the first British growers to take coals to Newcastle when they sold flowers in the Dutch flower auction in Aalsmeer. The business today regularly buys from the auctions in Holland to supplement their own produce and has expanded their wholesaling business which now runs four vans six days a week.

In 1996 the Hinckleys won the much coveted Hoff Classic Cup where judges voted their lilies the best from over seventy growers from around the world. Their policy is to produce smaller quantities of top quality produce for the discerning customer who values the best

Exemplifying all that's best in girls' education

One of Bedford's great benefactors of earlier times was Sir William Harpur, who began life as the son of a poor Bedford man and went on to become a prosperous London Merchant Taylor and, in 1561, Lord Mayor of London. Between 1552 and 1556 Sir William and his wife, Dame Alice, made a gift of money and land to the Corporation of Bedford. Sir William, no doubt remembering deprivations suffered during his own childhood, declared it his intention that the income from the land should be used for the benefit of the boys and girls of Bedford. Specifically, the objects of the Trust should be to provide for the maintenance of a Free School, for the nourishing and informing of poor boys of the town, and for the giving of marriage portions to poor maidens. This, of course, was perfectly in keeping with the thinking of the times - that boys were best served by a good education, and girls by a good marriage. Over the next three centuries a number of changes were introduced to the administration and management of the Trust, but the provision of higher education for girls

Above: Mrs McDowall, the school's first headmistress.
Right: The school as it appeared when it opened.
Below: The opening ceremony of the Science Block in May 1927.

continued to be overlooked; however, this deficiency was eventually spotted by the Royal Commission of Inquiry into Endowed Schools which was set up in 1866. Its report advocated, among other things, the establishing a High School for girls. As a result a new set of regulations was drawn up to govern the Harpur Trust, and these regulations received the Royal Assent in 1873.

The High School for Girls opened on Monday 8th May, 1882. There were 43 pupils, allocated between Forms I to V. The Headmistress, Mrs McDowall, was assisted by four mistresses, an art master, a singing master, a music master, and - somewhat surprisingly to a modern reader - a Sergeant Campbell who taught drill. He was soon replaced by Miss Stansfield who was the pioneer of modern gymnastics and went on to found the renowned Bedford PE College. The following year there were 87 pupils, and by 1898 there were over 600. Mrs McDowall sadly died within five months of the school's opening, after giving birth to a son, and it fell to her successor, Miss Belcher, to guide the School through its formative years; the legacies she has left include a fine Hall and the organ within it, and, perhaps most important of all,

the ethos of 'earnest, thoughtful study' in conjunction with the development of personal responsibility and the fulfilment of individual potential. The high standards which she set have been perpetuated by successive generations, resulting in the academic excellence for which the School is renowned today.

Bedford High School for Girls was built on the site of almshouses which were maintained by the Harpur Trust during the 19th century. It still occupies its original site, although the building has of course been extended and continually updated to meet constantly growing educational demands. The High School is renowned for its friendly atmosphere. There are today more than 850 pupils, who come from a wide variety of backgrounds; a proportion take advantage of the school's boarding facilities. Girls can enter the Junior School from the age of seven. Senior School pupils, between the ages of 11 and 16, benefit from a full and diverse range of subject options which are not confined to the National Curriculum but include traditional academic disciplines such as Latin and Greek, as well as the latest applications of computer literacy. In the Sixth Form, girls can choose from A and AS level subjects to meet virtually every possible demand, and can also take additional GCSE and non-examination courses of general interest. A programme of Personal

and Social Education complements the academic curriculum, and throughout the School the girls are encouraged to participate fully in an extensive and imaginative variety of teams, clubs and societies which cater for every conceivable interest, from the Duke of Edinburgh Awards Scheme to skiing, and from madrigal singing to rowing (the School is in fact recognised as one of the top rowing schools in the country). Dance is another area in which the School has established a reputation for excellence; and a unique combination of traditional excellence and the latest technology means that not only do music lovers have an opportunity to play in numerous orchestras and ensembles, but they can also experiment with synthesisers and sound processors, while young artists can use the latest computer design facilities in the setting of the original Victorian art studios where the talented painter Dora Carrington, perhaps the School's most controversial 'old girl', once worked.

Recent research has proved that girls educated in a single-sex school gain confidence, develop wide interests and take full leadership roles in every sphere. Pupils of Bedford High School for Girls can reap all these benefits while still enjoying joint activities, such as debating, drama, music and outdoor activities with the two Harpur Trust boys schools. Bedford High School is an excellent example of all that is best in girls education today; throughout its long history it has maintained an enviable reputation for outstanding academic achievement, and this, together with its well-founded traditions of all-round excellence, will continue far into the future.

Above left: *The visit of King George V and Queen Mary in June 1918.* ***Top:*** *Miss Holmes with her form, The Cambridge Sixth in 1895.*

Fuelling success in Bedford

The Watson family business was started shortly after the marriage of Kenneth and Irene Watson, and has remained very much a family concern ever since. Prior to launching this venture Ken, a former Chief Petty Officer in the Royal Navy, had worked for a couple of years as a mechanic, first for the London Brick Company at Stewartby and then for the GPO. Then in 1947 the couple bought a small garage in Houghton Conquest and equipped it as a workshop where Ken could put his mechanical skills to good use.

Local farmers brought their agricultural machinery in to Ken for repair, and all kinds of people brought in cycles, and by the mid-50s a lot were bringing their lawnmowers too, during the summer months. In 1957 Ken saw an opportunity to diversify, and began delivering paraffin in his Morris LD. His system was simple: if a customer wanted paraffin, he left his empty cans out, and Ken replaced these with full cans. This gave rise to the slogan 'Don't carry the can - let me deliver', which some readers might remember from the national advertising campaign for pink paraffin.

K Watson became a limited company in 1958, and it was around this time that Ken also began delivering Calor Gas. By this time the firm was growing, and Ken and Irene, who had until then run the business between them, were joined by Ken's brother David, who took care of the Calor Gas sales and deliveries. Also, the business needed more storage and work space. This problem was solved by building a new garage and workshop opposite the original premises; the firm moved to its new site, which included a car sales garage and a petrol station, in 1960, and in the same year it opened a hardware store in Ampthill, which it kept until 1997.

The firm's next diversification was into coal. This began in 1964 when Ken started buying coal in bulk, putting it into smaller bags and retailing it pre-packed. At first the coal was transferred to the

Below: An aerial view of the Houghton Conquest premises in the 1960s.
Bottom: The 1960s fleet.

working for the family firm in 1967; and Colin's brother Peter studied accountancy and joined the business in 1978 as a qualified accountant. David, meanwhile, was still running the Calor Gas dealership, selling cookers and appliances as well as bottled gas from premises in Brereton Road, and the coal business continued to thrive, expanding further afield into Norfolk in 1979.

Expansion continued throughout the 80s with the purchase of the company's current premises at Wilstead in 1983, and the construction of K Watson Commercials in 1988; the company had always carried out the servicing and repairs to its own vehicles, and now they took on an ERF franchise. Meanwhile on their industrial site at Wilstead on the outskirts of Bedford, two new buildings were erected and divided into units to be let, marking the beginning of the company's involvement in property management.

Today the business comprises K Watson Limited and its subsidiary K Watson Commercials Limited which services ERF and other makes of trucks. The coal business was sold in 1991, but the firm's 40-year association with Calor continues, and its activities as a Calor Gas principal dealer across the county account for a significant part of the firm's business. Haulage work continues to expand, with around 20 bulk tippers and an annual turnover well in excess of £1 million; and property investment remains on the agenda, with further site development is planned.

Ken, the founder, sadly died in 1988, and his brother retired in 1998 after 35 years with the company. Amazingly, after 50 years Irene continues to play an active part in the daily running of the business, together with Linda, Peter and his wife Julie who look after K Watson Limited and Colin and his wife Lynda who look after K Watson Commercials.

Above left: Kenneth Watson, founder of the company. Top: Today's fleet.

plastic sacks by hand, but later a machine was bought for the purpose. Ken then began selling wholesale to smaller coal merchants, and in 1965 the firm bought its first tipper lorry. Coal was proving a very successful venture for the firm and K Watson became one of the largest independent distributors in the South East; but, like repairing lawnmowers, it was seasonal. To compensate for the lack of trade during the summer, K Watson began hauling aggregates, and the firm's fleet of vehicles continued to grow. Over the years the fleet has included a Bedford TK, various Atkinson and Seddon Atkinson vehicles, an S80 Foden with a Tasker tipping trailer, Volvos and, of course, the ERFs which it runs today.

By 1965 Ken and Irene's children were old enough to make themselves useful in the business. Daughter Linda came to work in the office in 1965 and is still there today; son Colin followed in his Dad's footsteps and, having trained as a engineer, started

Hatters for the home

Frank Wenham took the step of becoming his own boss in 1959 following years of experience working for a local furniture retailer. He and brother Eric set up in business together running a paint and wallpaper shop in Luton which they called Hatters, a name reflecting both Luton's oldest industry and its football team. An easy name to remember when looking for a telephone number or a shop front in such an area.

They soon opened a second shop, in Bedford, through all the vibrant colour changes that were part of home life in the Swinging Sixties. Remember the contrasting colour schemes that dazzled the eye when purple paint was matched with floral orange and yellow papers. Similar contrasts existed between the textiles of carpets and furnishings in an era where hessian as a wall covering had become popular amongst the 'dedicated leaders of fashion'. So many of these asked for furniture to complement Hatter's paints and papers that the firm started selling furniture as well.

After ten years in Luton the brothers expanded into the furniture business with a shop in Bedford. This was to be the start of a home furnishing empire with outposts as far afield as Cambridge, Rushden and St Neots by the early 1970s. The stock held has expanded from the original paints and wallpapers, the latter at one stage consisted of 40,000 different patterns, to include that of a fully fledged garden centre at Greyfriars.

Think of the tastes to be catered for in a rural area, with a largely urban clientele whose occupations range from farm and industrial workers, through London commuters to all those connected with a university town of World Heritage status. It's mind boggling.

TV programmes have moved from the joys of cooking to the variegated business of furnishing homes in ways that would leave the original builders and occupants flabbergasted at the sheer imagination of it all. Try running a business which successfully caters for that! Hatters do and do it well in keeping abreast of public tastes brought about by the design 'gurus' of today. Once upon a time ordinary people would look upon changing styles with the eyes of outsiders but today they are ready to change styles as soon as the fiery torch of fashion appears on their horizon.

Below: *An artist's impression of the firm's premises in the 1970s.* ***Bottom:*** *Wallpaper samples in the 1970s.*

Hatters succeed not just by stocking a huge selection of stylish, comfortable furniture but by understanding what people want to achieve in their homes and their lives. As a result the well trained staff are able to listen to customers, visualise the effect they seek and, in the light of their expertise, give sound advice to the buyer. Many of Hatters staff have a record of long service and well deserved promotion within the expanding company as regular customers will recognise as they see the people they trust moving up the ladder of success. When people put such a high proportion of their earnings into the place where they live what goes into furnishing and decorating their homes is of great importance.

Value for money and the 'Can we live with it?' quality are matters which Hatter's staff recognise as being uppermost in people's minds, whether they are making a complete room change or just buying one item to fit in with their existing decor.

The revolutions in public spending and tastes which have occurred during the forty years of Hatter's business are exemplified by the firm's closure of its town centre shops and expansion into the popular edge of town Retail Park on the Goldington Road. Here customers can park,

without hassle, at the door of Hatter's 50,000 square feet building, which contains the largest selection of quality furniture in the region. Since the 70s Paul Wenham and David Cooper, furnishers to a wide area, are the second generation to run the business. They are already joined by the third generation of Wenhams following the tradition of family service to their customers.

Ready for a change in the home that will cheer one up without breaking the bank? A visit to Hatters to view the enormous selection and to discuss one's needs with attentive knowledgeable staff will set the ball rolling.

Above and below: *The premises today.*

Pets, Fleets and Windows

If anyone wonders what the connection between this unlikely combination is, it's insurance. Everyone knows that people today can insure anything from their holiday activities, children's schooling and funerals to the weather on a sports day, the delivery of business equipment and anything else that comes to mind. As the advertisements once said 'strong stuff, this insurance' and 'get the strength of the insurance companies around you'. Today when insurance cover is required for a greater variety of eventualities than ever before most insurers still cater for the normal majority but there are esoteric specialists such as Philip A Barnes who cater for the unusual as well as the usual.

It is no surprise to discover that this insurance agency was founded in 1950 by an entrepreneurial musician who, no doubt, found the average insurance company unable to offer cover on his instruments. A thoroughly sound reason for starting up a new business to insure not only his own instruments but also those of countless musicians needing to insure the tools of their trade as they travelled and played. During the fifties and sixties dancers at every village 'hop', let alone dances in the 'Dujon' Assembly Rooms and posh hotels, danced to live dinner jacketed four piece bands. This was a tremendous market

Right and below: *A 'before and after' view of the firm's premises at Mill Street.*

for live wire Philip Barnes and Arthur Jones, his experienced Insurance Salesman partner.

The two partners set up shop in the High Street as insurance brokers at a time when many people dealt directly with insurance companies while those who had bank accounts asked their banks, or more rarely their solicitors, which insurance companies were trustworthy and long lasting. The growth of independent insurance brokers is a modern trend to which the public has responded with enthusiasm in its search for flexible, cost effective insurance schemes suitable for the man in the street.

Two years later Messrs. Barnes and Jones moved to Mill Street in which locality Philip Barnes has remained to this day moving from number 6 to 14 and finally to numbers 45/47.

The upsurge in business and prosperity that launched the New Elizabethan Age of the 1950s finally put to rest the long years of rationing, shortages and poverty of the past.

Insuring the homes of the Property Owning Democracy took off in a big way and as public and private investment in buildings such as the fast multiplying schools and factories, to mention the tip of the iceberg, expanded so, too, did the insurance world expand. Since those exciting days booms and recessions have come and gone but the disposable incomes of ordinary citizens have risen to levels undreamed of by earlier generations. It is this very prosperity which has led to Philip Barnes becoming specialists in its unique fields.

One of the growth industries of our times is that of Pet Care which has exploded in an animal loving nation. The range of pets has extended from the familiar 'mousers', originally kept to earn their keep by destroying vermin, and dogs, various, once kept to guard homes, premises and

families to include the exotic and delicate foreign species. Useful, that is edible, pet pigs and rabbits have been replaced by the ubiquitous guinea pigs, as eaten abroad, hamsters and gaudy insects, fish, birds and other animals, both harmless and too poisonous to touch. Not only is this Noah's Ark collection grist for the insurance mill but the owners of Pet Shops and Grooming Parlours need tailor made insurance schemes to cover their staff, premises, customers and livestock against loss, damage and possible outbreaks of disease around the clock.

Businesses of all kinds with company cars or other vehicles requiring specialist insurance cover tailored for their own circumstances look to Philip Barnes to broker deals. Even those whose fleets are barely a flotilla in size will find as square a deal as those with squadrons of vehicles at large.

Another modern business field is that of the plastic windows and double glazing units whose manufacturers and installers need specialist insurance to cover their unique products and services against all events and disasters other than Acts of God. Philip Barnes provide a professional service for all clients great and small.

Top: *A window display from 1970.*

Servicemen mix with civilians on High Street at the Mill Street and Silver Street crossroads in a picture dating from the 1940s.

Acknowledgments

Bedfordshire and Luton Archives and Records Service; special thanks to Mr Nigel Lutt and his colleagues of the Records Service for their contribution to the photographic content of the book. Most of the editorial images contained in this book were from the Bedford County Record Office Collection, original photographs from Beds. County Press; Mr Richard Wildman.

Thanks are also due to
Andrew Mitchell for penning the editorial text
and Margaret Wakefield and Mike Kirke for their copywriting skills